SCOTTISH NATIONALISM
at the
CROSSROADS

For my parents.

SCOTTISH NATIONALISM at the CROSSROADS

ROGER LEVY

SCOTTISH ACADEMIC PRESS
EDINBURGH

Published by
Scottish Academic Press Ltd
139 Leith Walk
Edinburgh EH6 8NS

SBN 7073 0595 0

British Library Cataloguing in Publication Data
Levy, Roger
  Scottish nationalism at the crossroads.
  1. Scotland. Nationalism
  I. Title
  320.5′4′09411

ISBN 0–7073–0595–0

Printed in Great Britain by
The Eastern Press Ltd
London and Reading

Table of Contents

Acknowledgements

This project has been long in the making, and I am indebted to numerous people, some of whom I have forgotten and others who would not thank me for naming them.

For the initial ideas, I would like to thank Daniel Latouche and Osvaldo Croci, formerly of McGill University, other colleagues in the political science department at McGill, and Professor Maurice Pinard of the sociology department. I am especially grateful to all those people who participated in the fieldwork interviews, for it was they more than anyone else who ensured that I really got started. I would also like to acknowledge the help given me by the cuttings libraries of the *Glasgow Herald* and *Daily Record* newspapers, and by the headquarters staff of the Scottish National Party.

Coming full circle, I owe special thanks to Jack Geekie of Bell College who made an invaluable contribution to the latter stages of the manuscript. Thanks also to Richard Rose and Jack Brand of Strathclyde University, Michael Keating of the University of Western Ontario and James Kellas of Glasgow University. My thanks to Cathy Wright and Anne Sharkey in the preparation of the manuscript, and to Margaret McCann and Jason Ditton for egging me on. Finally, I would like to thank my colleagues at Glasgow College for providing encouragement in the execution and completion of this project.

August, 1989   ROGER LEVY

Introduction

Until the Glasgow Govan by-election of November 1988, the 1980s was a decade best forgotten by supporters of Scottish nationalism and the Scottish National Party (S.N.P.). Starting in the late 1970s, the S.N.P. suffered a serious and continuing loss of support, and the consitutional issue, so much at the centre of political affairs between 1974 and 1979, receded in importance almost to vanishing point. Along with similar nationalisms elsewhere, it seemed that the nationalist movement in Scotland was entering a new ice age, banished to the fringes of political life.

The downturn in nationalist activity in the mature democracies also signalled a dwindling of academic interest in the phenomenon. After the post-mortems and obituaries, a half-finished structure of investigation remained, awaiting completion in the future. With the renewal of peripheral nationalism, building work has restarted. It is perhaps heartening that this is based on extensive foundations in the Scottish case.

The academic legacy consists of three main parts. At the most general level, the nationalist phenomenon in Scotland (and indeed elsewhere in the developed world), undermined the prevailing consensus concerning the integrative effects of a universal 'modernising' process. The widely held assumption that increasing cultural and political uniformity were the inevitable consequences of the spread of urban-industrial society from 'core' areas to the 'periphery' was challenged, most notably by Ernest Gellner (1969) and Michael Hechter (1975). Using the relationship between the constituent nations in the U.K. as his case study, Hechter argued that the modernisation process produced neither socio-economic nor cultural and political uniformity. On the contrary, pre-existing inequalities between core and peripheral areas became crystallised, resulting in the development of 'reactive' ethnic cleavages, and ultimately in the growth of political separatism.

Drawing heavily on this framework but coming to rather different conclusions, Nairn (1981) sought to explain Scotland's 'absent' nationalism in the age of European nationalism, and its appearance in the twilight era of the British imperial system. In contrast to Hechter, Nairn has argued that the key elite groups in Scotland were incorporated into the 'British' system at the outset, so preventing the development of political nationalism in Scotland. Yet others claimed that political separatism in Scotland was a consequence of the 'revolution of rising expectations' in the peripheries. As demands have been raised beyond the system's capacity to satisfy them, separatist movements have arisen to articulate the hopes of these communities [Hanham (1969), Birch (1978), Smith (1979), Mughan and McAllister (1982)].

Second, the changes in political behaviour entailed by the nationalist revival, and the motivations of nationalist voters provoked intense interest. Starting with Budge and Urwin's (1966) work on voting behaviour, the Scottish electorate has been analysed by social background, consumption behaviour, party and attitude. Much of the work has had a specifically nationalist focus – namely, the nationalist electorate itself or the nationalism of the electorate generally. However, the debate has impinged on many of the general assumptions contained in theories of voting behaviour, and has been central to the discussion of the changing character of the British electorate.

Finally, there was a renewed interest in the structural and institutional framework of political separatism at the national and sub-national levels. This literature is perhaps most developed within the context of Canadian federalism where it has a long pedigree in both official and academic circles. However, the appearance of Kellas's (1973) work on the Scottish political system, the Royal Commission on the Constitution (1973) and the debate surrounding devolved government for Scotland marked an important stage in the development of this form of inquiry in the U.K. and Scottish contexts.

While this study impinges on all those areas to a greater or lesser degree, its main focus is the S.N.P. and the forces governing the behaviour of the party since the early 1970s. Surprisingly, much less attention has been devoted to party behaviour than voter behaviour, and no major scholarly work on the nationalist movement in Scotland has been published since 1978. It is the objective of this study to help remedy this deficiency.

This book is not simply a detailed chronology of events inside the S.N.P. since the 1970s, although it is that too. It attempts to locate the S.N.P. within the party system, assesses the appeal of the party to the electorate and analyses the strategy and tactics of the nationalists on a number of key issues through the medium of a coherent behavioural framework. In order to achieve this, some of the best-known literature on party strategy has been adapted to suit the particular circumstances of the S.N.P.'s recent growth cycle. Using this framework, we will identify the particular constraints which inhibited the adoption of so-called 'rational' vote-winning strategies by the party during the 1970s, and trace through the consequences of this behaviour in the party's subsequent development.

The first section of the book is divided into two parts, the first of which concerns a theory of S.N.P. development and an analysis of the party's organisational characteristics. The second part reviews the S.N.P.'s electorate and the general strategy of the party until the early 1970s.

The next section of the book deals with the two main issues dominating the party's growth cycle – 'Scottish' oil and devolution. On oil, the evidence presented shows that despite exceptionally favourable circumstances, powerful constraints ultimately operated to blunt the effectiveness of the party's campaign. On devolution, the situation proved to be far more difficult. The party never quite managed to achieve a stable and credible strategy – the reverse in fact. The latter both exemplified and exacerbated internal conflict, and resulted in a downward spiral which culminated in the purges and recriminations of the 1979–82 period.

Interwoven with the evaluation of the S.N.P.'s campaign strategies on these two issues is an analysis of the party's internal dynamics. The working out of forces set in motion during the mid-1970s is examined in the third section of the book, which comprises the chapters on factionalism and reconstruction. The period between 1979 and 1982 represented the darkest years in the party's recent history, in which destructive processes returned the party to the status of a fringe organisation. The party underwent almost continual fragmentation and shrinkage, as contending factions competed for what was left of the organisation.

The legacy of this period is evident in the long and hesitant process of reconstruction which has been going on since 1982–83. We examine this however not in isolation, but in the context of the remarkable developments which have been taking place in the Labour Party in Scotland since 1979. The argument that the Labour Party has become more 'nationalist' is now common currency. We document the nature of that transformation and show how the Labour Party has moved to a position on devolution which is very similar to that taken by the S.N.P. in the 1970s, indeed similar to that taken by most 'home rule' nationalist movements since the 1940s.

The establishment of the Scottish Constitutional Convention is but the apex of this phenomenon. If a new separatist coalition is in the making, the question arises of its future role and development in the post-Govan era. The relationship between Labour and

S.N.P., and the likely consequences of these parties' present policy stances are examined in the concluding chapter, along with a summary and evaluation of the S.N.P.'s development over the whole period under study.

CHAPTER 1

The S.N.P. and the Party System

Nationalism has many incarnations – linguistic, cultural, literary and sporting to name a few. In one sense or another, Scotland has never been lacking in nationalism. However, as Nairn (1981) has argued, the development of political nationalism in the form of a modern nationalist movement has occurred relatively recently.[1] The distinction between Scottish nationalism as a political movement and the S.N.P. is still unclear, perhaps deliberately so in the context of Nationalist ideology, and necessarily so in the context of the origins of the party. The lateness of this development has not prevented its historical and political documentation however. The process of the formation of the S.N.P. out of two existing parties and a small band of nationalist activists has been well-documented by Webb (1977), Brand (1978) and others, as has the nature of party ideology and the growth of its organisation.[2]

Yet this does not allow a complete understanding of why the S.N.P. behaves in the way it does. As a contemporary political party, its actions must be reviewed within a wider contextual framework. The S.N.P. is a particular type of party operating in a particular type of party system. As a player in the electoral marketplace, it is in competition for votes with other organisations, although not necessarily on equal terms with them. Its organisational capabilities – generally viewed as an asset by serious students of the party – have to be seen in a comparative and developmental perspective, to reveal their constraining as well as enabling aspects. Basing the analysis on well-known theories of the party system and party competition, it will be argued that the S.N.P. is a classic example of a 'third' party, and as such, has faced problems in achieving sustained growth which are endemic to its status.

Distinguishing the S.N.P. as a 'third' party in the first instance is only possible within the framework of an agreed ranking or positional system however. The most well-known positional typology for parties in elective democracies is Duverger's (1954), which distinguishes between majority, major and minor parties. The S.N.P. certainly does not qualify as either a major or majority party in this schema. According to Duverger, both majority and major parties form governments, with majority parties enjoying regular and absolute parliamentary majorities and major parties usually seeking coalition partners. Minor parties on the other hand, 'are makeweights whether in office or opposition'.[3] This particular category covers a very wide range of parties from the electorally and organisationally insignificant to mass parties participating in coalition governments. Thus, Duverger makes a further distinction based on organisational and social characteristics between different types of minor party, and introduces the new category of the medium party. The latter is typically a coalition partner of a major party in government or opposition (e.g. the German Free Democrats, F.D.P.).

In this sense, the medium party is an intermediary or broker between the major parties. This specialised definition might be applied to third parties in order to differentiate them from minor parties. In this case however, it would exclude all those parties in 'two party' simple majority systems, which perform quite well electorally, are usually referred to as third parties, but secure only minimal parliamentary representation (e.g. the old British Liberal Party and the Liberal–S.D.P. Alliance, the Canadian New Democrats). Such parties seldom enter government, principally because coalitions are either rare (as in the Westminister system since 1945), or impossible (as in Presidential systems).

A medium party could alternatively be conceived as simply intermediate between major and minor parties in terms of electoral performance and organisational strength. This would then take in the most well-known examples of 'third' parties in two party systems; indeed, much of the literature does suggest that such parties are peculiar to two party systems. Epstein (1967), specifically excludes 'fairly large minority parties operating in multiparty systems' from his definition of third parties, which are those parties which 'regularly break the two party competitive pattern by winning or threatening to win enough offices to influence control of the government'.[4]

The most interesting aspect of this definition is the key capacity of third parties to influence the majority parties. This model is followed by Rosenstone et al. (1984) in the U.S. case, and Sartori (1976) in reference to the significance of minor parties. The difficulty with this idea lies in its imprecision. The concept of 'influence' is neither concisely defined nor is any suggestion made as to how it might be quantified. The Epstein model suggests that third party influence is a function of electoral performance. This could have two meanings: either the third party holds the balance of power in the legislature and has direct influence over the government, or the size and distribution of the third party vote influences the outcome of the election to the detriment of one party and the advantage of another.

Epstein seems to adopt the first meaning, citing examples from Canadian provincial politics, to which could be added Liberal–Country Party coalitions in Australia, the Lib–Lab 'pact' in Britain in 1977 and the various F.D.P. supported coalitions in Germany. There is no reason why the second meaning should be precluded however. Electoral attainment above a certain threshold can have a dramatic effect on outcomes. By skewing the distribution of legislative seats, the third party can have a tremendous influence on the size of the winning majority, as was shown for example by the performance of the Liberal–S.D.P. Alliance in 1983.

As this kind of influence is purely objective, it has no necessary behavioural consequences. From a behavioural point of view, third party influence is best defined as the ability to change the behaviour of a major party on the basis of perceived threat. In this case, third parties exercise influence at the programmatic level. As Rosenstone et al. argue, 'the power of third parties lies in their capacity to affect the content and range of political discourse and ultimately public policy . . . by raising issues and options which the major parties have ignored'.[5] This is particularly salient in the case of the S.N.P. and other ethno-nationalist parties, as regionalist demands have been incorporated into the programmes of major parties in the U.K., Canada and Spain arguably because of their influence.

If a positional definition of third parties is adopted which incorporates a number of these aspects – medium vote, medium size, infrequent participation in government, brokerage role, programmatic influence – the question arises as to what extent the S.N.P. satisfies these criteria. As the S.N.P.'s attempts to achieve programmatic influence will be assessed later, the discussion will be confined to the other aspects of the definition for the moment.

Compared to its main rivals in Scotland, the S.N.P. is exceptional in so far as it has never been a party of government. Even the Scottish Social and Liberal Democrats and the Social Democratic Party owe their collective lineage to two parties of government (the Liberal Party and the Labour Party). The only claim the

S.N.P. can make to office is the sporadic control of some local authorities since the 1960s. Even here, it has achieved majority control in only a very few cases. In this sense, it fits the model of a minor rather than a third party.

As far as electoral performance is concerned, the S.N.P. vote at general elections in Scotland between 1945 and 1987 can be separated into two distinct periods. Table 1 shows that between 1945 and 1966, it figured only as a minor party which had a negligible impact on electoral outcomes. Its share of the total vote was low and it did not contest all seats. The 1966 results did show that its support had significantly increased however, as the party achieved double figure averages in the seats it did contest. There was a profound transformation in the late 1960s with the party gaining notable by-election and local government successes in 1967 and 1968, and contesting almost all seats at the 1970 general election. Although a disappointment compared to the expectations in the party at the time, the S.N.P. share of the vote in 1970 showed a significant increase over the 1966 figure. Since 1970, the party's share of the vote has always reached double figures and it has always contested all seats in Scotland (except Orkney and Shetland). Since 1967, the party has returned at least one M.P. with a high point of 11 between October 1974 and May 1979.

Table 1

Percentage vote gained by party in Scotland General elections 1945–87

Election	Conservative	Labour	Liberal	S.N.P.	Turnout (%)
1945	41	48	5	1	69
1950	45	46	7	0	81
1951	49	48	3	0	81
1955	50	47	2	1	75
1959	47	47	4	1	78
1964	41	49	8	2	78
1966	38	50	7	5	76
1970	38	45	6	11	74
1974	33	37	8	22	79
1974	25	36	8	30	75
1979	31	42	9	17	77
1983	29	34	25	12	72
1987	24	42	19	14	73

In terms of electoral performance then, the S.N.P. achieved third party status by 1970 at the latest, and arguably as early as 1966. Although there was a hiatus in S.N.P. growth in 1969, and the party entered the 1970 election on a declining rather than a rising curve of support, this must be placed in the context of a ten year period of outstanding electoral and organisational improvement. The S.N.P. had made the transition from minor party to third party status during the latter part of the 1960s, and was poised for further growth, if not in the short term then certainly in the medium term future.[6]

This is not to say that either its vote or its representation have been equally significant at all times since 1970. Its most influential phase (1974–79) did qualify the S.N.P. as much more than simply a minor party, owing to a combination of factors rather than any single one taken in isolation. The S.N.P. not only achieved its highest ever share of the Scottish vote (30.4% in October 1974), but also returned its highest ever number of M.P.s in circumstances (a wafer thin Labour majority by courtesy of Labour's performance in Scotland), where it could exercise real leverage.

In terms of size, the S.N.P. increased from an organisation of a few hundred in the 1950s to perhaps 2,000 in 1962. From there on, it grew by almost geometric progression in the 1960s, attaining a membership of 20,000 in 1965, 42,000 in 1966 and 120,000 in 1968.[7] Although the figure has never subsequently reached this height, equally it has never slipped back to the levels of the early 1960s. Even in the dark days of 1983, the official estimate was 20,000. While there is some question over the accuracy of these figures, the same caveats apply to membership figures issued by other parties. The S.N.P.'s official size must be placed in context therefore. As the politically dominant party in Scotland (the Labour Party) has only some 20,000 individual members officially, at present the S.N.P. ranks easily as a significant political organisation.

Party Competition and Party Organisation

On most of these positional criteria then, the S.N.P. of the early 1970s can be classified as third party. The achievement of this status posed two essential problems common to all third parties – how to make the transformation to major party status, and how to avoid a reversion to minor party status. From the S.N.P.'s point of view, remaining a third party was neither satisfactory nor secure. As in other cases, the opportunities were great, but so were the risks of failure. It is of some importance therefore, to establish the general conditions under which a third party can grow, and to identify the resources it can use to do so. In Anthony Downs's (1957) basic model of party competition, there are two circumstances in which this might occur. Assuming a two party, simple majority system in which voters choose those parties which advantage them most and there is a normal distribution of voter preferences, support for 'third' parties will increase if there is either a major redistribution of voter preferences (through an extension of the franchise for example), or where one or both major parties drift away from the 'centre'.[8]

As critics have argued, Downs made many assumptions for the purposes of model-building, not the least of which were about parties themselves. He viewed them as rational organisations concerned solely with vote maximisation, and run by office seekers. Thus, while it was possible that aggregate voter preferences could alter, it was unlikely that parties would drift away from the 'centre' unless the voters did (assuming they were in this one-dimensional space in the first place). Given that Downs's view of parties was based on U.S.-style Presidential coalitions, his assumptions were hardly surprising. Alternative assumptions concerning the organis-ational dynamics of parties were not taken into account, nor perhaps could they have been in the framework of Downs's theoretical enterprise.

Leaving aside all the other contentious assumptions Downs makes, this notion has been challenged by many of Downs's critics, most notably Hirschman (1970) and Robertson (1976).[9] Hirschman makes a very simple modification to Downs's schema by adding an extra category of political actors, namely the party activists, and applying Downs's logic to the resultant party system. In contrast to voters, Hirschman argues that party activists tend to be located at the ideological extremes, and have a vested interest in the organisations they belong to (in terms of participation, office holding etc.). They are therefore much less likely than voters either to 'defect' to the opposition or lapse into inactivity.[10] Thus, instead of the major parties tending to coalesce around the 'centre', they will tend instead to drift towards their ideological extremes. If this is the case, then opportunities for third party growth arise assuming voter preferences stay the same.

Taking into account differences in party systems (hence electoral arrangements), and party organisation, there will be variations in the strength of this tendency. At the systemic level, it will be weakest in multi-party systems because activists can defect to a variety of neighbouring parties at little ideological 'cost' to themselves, and strongest in two party systems where the ideologi-cal distance between the main parties is relatively great. At the organisational level, it will be weakest in parties where activists are a relatively feeble influence on office-seeking leaders, and strongest where activists are comparatively powerful.

If this is the case, then two party systems where the major parties are under comparatively strong activist influence seem to be most at risk from ideological drift and successful third party growth. However, this takes no account of the disabling problems created by the organisational structures of most third parties. As Robertson (1976) argues, third parties in such systems are likely to be under even greater activist control than the major parties simply because they are formed later historically. Thus, Robertson's 'emerging' parties tend to encourage activism, while his 'mature' parties tend to put a much greater value on winning or retaining office. Whatever advantages third parties may have in terms of manoeuvrability are thus balanced by the disadvantages of greater activist control, and their lack of governing experience, a fatal flaw in Robertson's view.

Robertson's typology in fact resembles Duverger's distinction between 'mass' and 'cadre' parties, although in Duverger's account, mass parties do not always encourage 'activism', and cadre parties are not without activists.[11] If Duverger's organisational characterisation of the branch party is added on to the mass party model however, then Robertson's emerging party concept becomes clear. As Duverger observed, these parties are characterised by a relatively open organisational structure in comparison to cell and cadre parties. In practice, this means that there will be few if any conditions placed on membership, and members will have multiple opportunities to participate in party affairs through the proliferation of elections, elected offices and policy processes involving balloting and discussion. His description of a party as a 'collection of communities, a union of small groups dispersed throughout the party (branches, caucuses, local associations etc.) and linked together by co-ordinating institutions' is nowhere more appropriate than in the context of the mass based branch party which, he remarks, allows 'of only a slack, superficial and intermittent discipline'.[12]

This does not mean that the generality of party members are meaningfully involved in the decision making process. As Duverger argues, mass parties are not necessarily democratic and those which are democratic and open in structure do not necessarily engender mass participation. Dependence on the mass membership for logistical support, and formal adherence to participatory ideals may conceal a magic circle of activists and activism. As more general studies of political participation have shown, there is a taxonomy of participation which ranges from, say, voting in national elections to running for the highest political office in the land. The intensity of participation bears an inverse relationship to the numbers of those participating. Thus, in the context of the mass branch party, the taxonomy would be roughly as follows:

Figure 1
Participation in political parties

LEVEL OF PARTICIPATION	TYPE OF PARTICIPATION	NOS. PARTICIPATING
Low	Payment of subscriptions Vote in party elections Attend local meetings	high
Medium	Campaign for party Stand for local party office Attend national meetings Candidate for public office	medium
High	Stand for national party office	low

The intensity of participation within a party therefore depends on how sharply participation falls off at each level of the taxonomy, and on how much it is judged necessary to participate in order to be meaningfully involved. While open and democratic procedures provide opportunities for participation, they do not guarantee it. The commitment in time and energy which they entail may find few takers. Thus, the high levels of internal competition endemic to such procedures do not necessarily involve vast numbers of party members directly. They are more likely to participate indirectly, as the working of the activist 'career system' (Sartori 1976) exacts its price.[13]

This system is not simply analogous to the static leader–activists dichotomy posed by either Hirschman or Robertson. The process of career advancement inside parties through the mustering of votes (Sartori 1976), or what Waldman (1972) describes as 'the mutually profitable exchanges between political entrepreneurs and party members'[14] is dynamic, and creates a perennial instability in the policy process as incumbents and contenders compete for party offices and nominations by constructing a series of predatory alliances. This is likely to show itself in the form of factional activity and a high turnover of office holders as the balance of power between them changes.

In this model, the party itself is a marketplace in which competition for position and influence is loosely regulated by the internal constitution of the organisation. The aspirations of individual party members are the commodities of exchange in a system which extends from local to national level. Policy is not so much the outcome of a conflict between the 'activists' and the 'office seekers', but rather is the product of a series of incumbent–contender conflicts within the career system. The transition from 'activist' to 'office seeker' is neither complete nor final because competition will cast contenders and incumbents into different roles. As Schlesinger (1965) argues however, there is a tendency for the balance to shift as individuals seek higher office.[15]

Ideology does play a role in these conflicts. Ideological deviations from accepted party canon by elected party office holders or parliamentary representatives are undoubtedly important in stirring the broth. But these must be placed in an organisational context which allows or even encourages intra-party conflict. The more favourable the environment from this point of view, the greater the conflict. Thus, policy will tend to be least stable and least voter oriented in those parties which combine a high level of structurally generated internal competition for office with a relatively large activist base. In this case, mass branch parties are at a disadvantage compared with cell and cadre parties, and mass branch parties which are also third parties are most disadvantaged of all because of their activist base and the participative bias of their constitutional arrangements. Electoral decline will bring additional factional activity as incumbents come under direct challenge for the party's failure.

However, internal competition arguably has a benign effect on party organisation so long as activist aspirations can be satisfied through electoral growth and increased opportunites for office holding. When parties are relatively new, increased opportunities for office holding are created as they expand electorally and geographically. Thus they may be immune from conflict until the organisational network reaches saturation point and electoral performance peaks. If they cannot be transformed into less internally competitive organisations at this point, then these disruptive forces may wipe out whatever gains have been achieved.

The question is why third parties invariably tend to adopt such a manifestly unstable organisational form in competitive democracies. The answer is to be found in the reliance such parties place on their members for organisational and financial sustenance. In exchange for this, members receive multiple opportunities for candidature and participation in the decision making process of the party. Electoral growth thus presupposes organisational growth and membership involvement. The idea of linking organisational change to electoral performance is hardly new. Epstein (1967), Rokkan (1970), Wellhofer (1972, 1979) and Bartolini (1985) all stress the importance of organisational variables in building the competitive position of certain types of mass parties, in particular social democratic ones.[16] Following Epstein's analysis of European Socialist parties, Wellhofer suggests that new parties attract voters in the early stages by a process of 'organisational encapsulation' which incorporates them into party structures, typically at the local or 'branch' level. New party units are thus built in tandem with the expansion of the electoral base until an organisational saturation point is reached beyond which there is stagnation followed by conflict and decline. Wellhofer estimates that this process accounted for 25% of the rate of change in popular support for the Norwegian and Argentinian Socialist parties in the post war period.[17]

The neo-nationalist parties that grew so rapidly in the 1960s arguably had to use exactly the same methods, and consequently suffered from the same cyclical tendencies. Caveats notwithstanding, it will be argued that the S.N.P. has sought, and indeed still seeks to achieve electoral growth by the same means, and has an organisational structure which resembles this model in its essential aspects. While a source of greater strength at times, the party's organisational dynamics have had a profoundly negative impact on its performance at others as subsequent chapters will show.

S.N.P. organisation: two views

Like other parties of a similar type, the role of the individual member is potentially much greater in the S.N.P. compared to its larger rivals. Notwithstanding variations in membership size over the years, the S.N.P. has adopted a mass party format which places no restrictions on individual membership and relies on members for financial and logistical support. It is structured so as to allow, even encourage, membership participation. There are more opportunities for individual participation via elections and ballots in comparison to the Conservative Party, and the individual is accorded a greater role than is the case in the Labour Party, as elections are conducted solely on the principle of one member one vote.

The local organisation of the party – branches and constituency associations – is decentralised insofar as membership lists and subscriptions are held and collected locally rather than nationally. National and local units are linked together by elective and representative processes, with the party's National Executive Council (N.E.C.), originating from three distinct sources – the parliamentary group, elections from an intermediate assembly (the

National Council), and elections from conference representatives. All party office holders (as distinct from employees), are elected by delegates to the annual conference.

The National Council, in so far as it acts as co-policy maker with the annual conference, has no real counterpart in either the Labour or Conservative parties. Consisting of the nominees of local parties and members elected by the annual conference, it gives the localities a potentially strong voice in policy making, as the local representatives are dominant numerically. In addition to the National Council, the S.N.P. has a consultative National Assembly (more akin to the Conservative Party's National Council) made up of local and national representatives, plus a variable number of ad hoc national policy committees. Thus, as in other third parties in the U.K., there are, arguably, significantly more opportunities for participation in decision making and office holding at the intermediate level in the S.N.P. compared to the major parties.

The emphasis on individual membership is also shown in the process for selecting parliamentary candidates, where selection is based on the principle of one member one vote, a claim which cannot be made by either the Labour or Conservative parties. While actual participation in any of these activities by the vast majority of party members may indeed be fairly low, the fact remains that individual members do have multiple opportunities to participate. The failure to use these opportunities should not be confused with their absence.

Such is the formal structure of the party in brief, and the position of the individual member within it. However, this should not necessarily be taken to be its organisational reality. According to Crawford's (1982) comprehensive study of the S.N.P.'s internal workings, the party's organisation has been the subject of only limited debate. Apart from this work, Mansbach's local study (1972), Brand's (1978) chapter on the organisation of the party in the mid-1970s and Kauppi's article on the party's decline (1982), stand as landmarks in a pretty empty field.[18] There is nevertheless a sharp disagreement on the nature of the party's organisation and the participation of members in it.

Until the Crawford study, the prevailing consensus was that behind the formal structure, the S.N.P. was a highly decentralised mass branch type party, with a strong emphasis on local autonomy and membership participation. Mansbach (1972) concluded that the S.N.P. was 'fundamentally . . . a branch or local dominated party', and Brand (1978), remarking on the financing of the party argues that 'the S.N.P. was by far the most mass orientated political movement in Scotland. Since concentration of these mass contributions is at the lowest level of the branch, the financial base of the movement is very much at the grass roots'.[19]

The only real disagreement was over how effective the organisation could be in these circumstances. According to Mansbach, many of the party's difficulties in mounting a national campaign flowed directly from its 'decentralised' structure, terminology which was in his view little more then a euphemism for chaos and confusion:

> The lack of party discipline, the democratic mode of election to high office, the decentralised direction and lack of co-ordination in party affairs and the localist concerns of branch leaders prepared the party to compete successfully in local contests, but not to mobilise for a general election.[20]

Mansbach's study of the S.N.P.'s local organisation in 1969 found that communications were poor both horizontally and vertically, and that party H.Q. was inefficient and disorganised. With few constraints on branch activity and a high turnover of elected national officers, central direction was almost non-existent. So although the party had attracted many new members, it was incapable of mobilising them.

The later accounts of Webb (1977), Brand (1978) and Mullin (1979) are far less pessimistic about the party's capabilities, which is quite understandable in view of the successes which had been achieved since Mansbach's study. While still maintaining that the party was highly decentralised, Webb does suggest that the central leadership was gaining greater national authority and improved organisational efficiency as a result of limited reform.[21] Brand makes a similar case in his detailed account of S.N.P. organisation, but argues that the rapid expansion of the number of branches and members in the 1970s made central control extremely difficult even if the intention was to strengthen it.[22]

The 'decentralist' argument is indirectly strengthened by Mishler and Mughan's study (1978) of Scottish M.P.s. This showed that S.N.P. M.P.s claimed to devote more time to constituency work than M.P.s from any other party, thus indicating a continuing preoccupation with local issues as a result, perhaps, of pressure from local branches and constituency associations.

The alternative thesis advanced by Crawford is that the S.N.P. had become a highly centralised party by the middle of the 1960s in which the mass membership played little part in decision making. He argues that the centralisation of organisational matters (which are defined as management, tactics and strategy), was an imperative which was necessary if the party was to achieve electoral success. The fact that it was successful in the 1970s only proved that centralisation had occurred. The commitment to community politics and the influence of the membership via the National Council on general policy questions are explained as essentially a function of the party's dependence on local funding arrangements. But on the important issues, decisions were made by a core ruling group whose composition changed little over fourteen years.[23]

Communications in the party corresponded to a top down rather than a bottom up model. Even in the National Council, which is identified as the main forum for membership participation in national affairs, members tended to be recipients of information rather than communicators of it.[24] The overall impression therefore is one of an increasingly tightly managed party, with power concentrated in the hands of a few senior figures who consituted an informal ruling group within the N.E.C. Crawford argues that this particular body, strengthened by the internal reforms of the 1960s, was effectively able to dominate the party. In contrast to Brand, Crawford does not see the expansion of the membership as a hindrance to leadership power: on the contrary, this growth required the sacrifice of the 'participatory ideals' of the party.[25]

The whole notion of membership 'opinion' and who makes it is central to the debate about participation, and in the S.N.P.'s case there is much circumstantial evidence to support Crawford's centralist argument. For example, the Treasurer's report to the party's National Council in September 1973 suggests that opinion makers were few indeed, and that the party was less dynamic at the local level than many have suggested. Noting that two thirds of branches had not yet paid their subscriptions to headquarters, the Treasurer observed that his own branch was 'fairly typical in that there are approximately five or six active members'.[26] If this figure is generalised, then there would be a maximum of about 3,000 activists out of a total party membership of perhaps 80,000 in 1973. This hardly gives the impression of a vibrant or even truculent mass membership articulating sustained policy arguments.

As Crawford's study only covers the period until 1974, it does not consider the impact on the organisation of a high profile parliamentary group of unprecedented size. That the election of first seven, and then eleven, S.N.P. M.P.s in February and October 1974 respectively, was problematic for the party is not at issue. Mullin (1979) noted that in the space of just four years, 'there had been increasingly open conflict within the S.N.P. between the M.P.s, the N.E.C. and the branches on (devolution) and many

other issues).[27] Miller (1981) points out that the policies pursued
by the parliamentary group in 1977 and 1978 made it difficult for
the S.N.P. to build local coalitions with the Labour Party.[28] Does
this invalidate Crawford's argument and confirm the decentralist
case therefore?

A third view which can be adduced for the conflict does not
really confirm either organisational model. It rather suggests an
alternative model of elite domination and structural bifurcation.
While this view incorporates the centralist argument on the role
of the mass membership, it suggests that the leadership was part
of a broader decision-making elite, the diverse structure of which
was further complicated by the addition of the parliamentary
group. Because of the multiple opportunities for some kind of
participation in decision making at national level, those who were
so minded could probably find a forum for their views. If they
were not members of the N.E.C. (entry into which could be
secured by at least three routes), then they could seek membership
of the National Council which met on a quarterly basis with the
national office bearers to discuss policy. Even those candidates
who failed to get elected onto the National Council at annual
conference could still participate by securing a branch or constituency nomination. The party's annual conference and National
Assembly provided additional sites for conflict within the activist
elite.

Decision-making was neither quick nor decisive in this milieu.
This meant that the decision makers had not prepared for the
political consequences of parliamentary representation. Mullin
claims that the S.N.P. M.P.s never enjoyed the kind of authority
in their own party that Labour and Conservative M.P.s did,
because the it had never given much thought to its parliamentary
strategy.[29] It had been the official view since 1968 that the party's
capture of a majority of seats in Scotland constituted a mandate
for independence. The role of nationalist M.P.s was to sue for
independence once this stage had been reached. What they were
supposed to do in the meantime however, was unclear. Such was
the situation between 1974 and 1979.

Secondly, the party was not prepared for the organisational
consequences of parliamentary representation, and in particular
its effect of creating a bicephalous leadership. No prior arrangements had been made to secure a formal consultative framework
between the N.E.C. and the M.P.s, and later attempts to do so
proved less than successful. This particular problem may have
been avoided if the swings of electoral fortune had placed all the
party's leading figures in Parliament. Most of them failed to get

elected however, and many of those that were returned to Westminister were previously obscure or unknown figures in the party. For example, George Reid, S.N.P. M.P. for Clackmannan and East Stirling, had been a member of the Labour Party until two months before his election in February 1974.

But if the parliamentary group lacked many of the party's *de facto* leaders, then equally the party did not seek to incorporate the new M.P.s into the official leadership. If we look at the election by annual conference of national office bearers, there seems to have been little inclination to elect the new M.P.s to these positions between 1974 and 1979:

Table 2
Party office holders elected by annual conference, 1975–79

Year	Non M.P.s	M.P.s & former M.P.s	Total	Total no. of M.P.s
1975	11	1	12	11
1976	11	1	12	11
1977	11	1	12	11
1978	11	1	12	11
1979	7	5	12	3*

(*including one Member of European Parliament)[30]

Although it has to be said that not many M.P.s were nominated between 1975 and 1978, this perhaps only reinforces the view that the leadership was split between two centres. This cannot be blamed simply on the voting behaviour of conference delegates and the nominating branches and constituency associations. Existing office bearers could have taken practical steps toward integration by stepping down in favour of M.P. nominees or of ensuring that at least one or two of the major national offices were reserved for M.P.s. The M.P.s did have seven reserved places on the N.E.C. (an ad hoc arrangement that followed the February election), but this did not involve them in any party 'popularity poll' either at national conference or in the National Council. Their 'mandate' was thus distinct from that enjoyed by the elected national office bearers.

The distancing of themselves from the directing hand of the N.E.C. by the M.P.s is shown in Mishler and Mughan's (1978) study. 50% of S.N.P. M.P.s saw themselves as parliamentarians in the Burkean tradition, with none considering themselves as mere party delgates. Only 10% (one in other words) identified themselves as 'party loyalists', whereas 40% thought of themselves as 'propagandists'.[31] As they also seem to have been extremely active parliamentarians and constituency representatives, it could be inferred that their contacts with the national leadership in Scotland must have been quite limited. Thus, Mullin argues that as the party in Scotland demanded more accountability from the M.P.s, they demanded 'the right to act independently'.[32]

This does not mean that the M.P.s were in conflict with the whole of the party, as the evidence suggests that the primary site of conflict between the M.P.s and the party was in the N.E.C. The N.E.C. instructed the parliamentary group without success on at least one occasion to take a certain course of action, and there was a series of other conflicts between the two bodies as already noted. The existence of a broader elite merely added to these difficulties by multiplying the points at which conflict could occur, and adding to the pressures which could be exerted by one leadership group to the other. The quarterly meetings of the National Council for example, became increasingly important sites for conflict between rival leader factions as policy disagreements came into the open, first over devolution and then over the very direction of the party.

As we have argued, conflict might have been avoided either through the fortuitous election to parliament of the existing leaders in 1974, or through structural change at leadership level after 1974. In the longer term, a harmonisation of the leadership might have been achieved. If we look at the political background of prospective parliamentary candidates in 1970, October 1974 and 1979, we can see that there was an unmistakable tendency for the level of experience of party office in its broadest sense to rise.

Table 3

S.N.P. Prospective Parliamentary Candidates: Previous political activity (% Candidates)[33]

	1970	1974	1979
Member only, less than five years	26	6	14
Member & local officer, less than five years	31	17	10
Local &/or national officer, over five years	23	51	27
Local &/or national officer, over ten years	20	27	49
(N =	65	71	71)

This suggests that the selective and centralising processes that had already taken place within the national leadership in the 1960s were now taking place among the parliamentary candidates in the 1970s. The elite which we have identified was thus becoming more homogeneous in terms of its experience. Had this happened earlier rather then later, the evident split between parliamentarians and national leaders might not have taken place, as there would have been a shared experience of leadership activity within the party. Instead, the period after 1974 showed an increasing level of internal rivalry which culminated in a breakdown in the decision making process at various points in 1978 and 1979, and the fractionalisation of the leadership after 1979.

As for structural change, various attempts were made to improve the relationship between the M.P.s and the rest of the leadership after 1974. The fact that a top level working group was set up in 1977 to define the basic ground rules suggests how little progress had actually been made. But even if these attempts had succeeded (which they did not), they would have only entailed improvements to the status quo through better communication and so on. A fundamental reform of party structures was not contemplated as an option. Thus, the structural pressures which created conflict remained.

The creation of the parliamentary group and its relationship with the rest of the party did indeed have a negative impact on the decision-making process in the S.N.P. The addition of the group sheds a particularly interesting light on the party's organisational character, as it further complicated what was already a complex and conflictual structure. However, this was not because of the existence of a highly active mass membership seeking to be involved. While party structures allowed for participation at national level, this was only for the elite who could muster either votes or nominations. Nevertheless, it was the cumbersome and fragmented nature of this elite which contributed to the failure to integrate the parliamentarians satisfactorily and to give them a clear role.[34]

Notes

[1] T. Nairn, *The Break-up of Britain: Crisis and Neo-Nationalism* (2nd edn.), London, New Left Books, 1981.
[2] See, for example, J. Brand, *The National Movement in Scotland*, London, Routledge, 1978; K. Webb, *The Growth of Nationalism in Scotland*, Harmondsworth, Penguin, 1978; I. McAllister, 'U.K. Nationalist Parties: One Nationalism or Three?', in P. Madgwick and R. Rose, (eds.), *The Territorial*

Dimension in U.K. Politics, London, Macmillan, 1982; J. Kellas, *Modern Scotland*, London, Pall Mall, 1968; H. J. Hanham, *Scottish Nationalism*, London, Faber, 1969; C. Harvie, *Scotland and Nationalism: A Study of Politics and Society in Scotland 1707–present*, London, Allen and Unwin, 1977.

³ M. Duverger, *Political Parties*, New York, Wiley, 1954, p. 288.

⁴ L. Epstein, *Political Parties in Western Democracies*, London, Pall Mall, 1967, p. 46.

⁵ S. J. Rosenstone, R. L. Behr, E. H. Lazarus, *Third Parties in America: Citizen Response to Major Party Failure*, Princeton, Princeton University Press, 1984, pp. 8–9.

⁶ Miller, using the literal meaning of 'third party', argues that the by-election results of 1970–74 suggested that 'the S.N.P. had replaced the Liberals as Scotland's third party, but they did not provide sound evidence to contradict indications that the S.N.P. was a weak third party'. W. Miller, *The End of British Politics? Scots and English Political Behaviour in the 1970s*, Oxford, Oxford University Press, 1981, p. 58.

⁷ Kellas (1984) gives S.N.P. membership figures for the period 1962–83 which shows that the party grew from 2,000 to 120,000 between 1962 and 1968. It had declined to 70,000 in 1971, rose to 85,000 in 1974 but was back at 20,000 in 1983. The earlier figures are partially confirmed by Mansbach's (1972) survey of 18% of branches in 1969 which suggested a total membership in excess of 100,000. Mansbach notes that 'party records at H.Q. were at best incomplete and disorganised'. J. G. Kellas, *The Scottish Political System* (3rd edn.), Cambridge, Cambridge University Press, 1984, p. 142; R. Mansbach, 'The S.N.P.: A revised profile', *Comparative Politics*, January 1973, pp. 185–210.

⁸ A. Downs, *An Economic Theory of Democracy*, New York, Harper, 1957.

⁹ D. Robertson, *A Theory of Party Competition*, New York, Wiley 1976; A. Hirschman, *Exit, Voice and Loyalty*, Cambridge, Harvard, 1970.

¹⁰ Hirschman, ibid., pp. 75–100.

¹¹ Duverger, *Political Parties*, pp. 63–71.

¹² Duverger, ibid., pp. 17 and 35.

¹³ G. Sartori, *Parties and Party Systems: A framework for analysis*, Cambridge, Cambridge University Press, 1976, p. 97.

¹⁴ S. Waldman, *Foundations of Political Action: An exchange theory of politics*, Boston, Little Brown, 1972, p. 24. See also R. L. Curry and L. L. Wade, *A Theory of Political Exchange: Economic Reasoning in Political Analysis*, New Jersey, Prentice Hall, 1968, Hirschman, *Exit, Voice and Loyalty*, and Robertson, *A Theory of Party Competition*.

¹⁵ See J. A. Schlesinger, *Ambition and Politics: Political Careers in the U.S.*, Chicago, Rand McNally, 1966. According to Von Beyme, incumbents tend to accumulate offices as they ascend the career structure, thus making competition even fiercer. K. Von Beyme, *Political Parties in Western Democracies*, Aldershot, Gower, 1985, p. 362.

¹⁶ Epstein, *Political Parties in Western Democracies*, pp. 117–118; E. Spencer Wellhofer, 'Dimensions of Party Development: A study in organisational dynamics', *Journal of Politics*, 1972, and E. Spencer Wellhofer, 'Strategies for party organisation and voter mobilisation; Britain, Norway and Argentina', *Comparative Political Studies*, 12, 2, 1979, pp. 169–203; S. Rokken (ed.), *Citizens, Elections and Parties*, Oslo, Universitetsforlaget, 1970, S. Bartolini, 'The membership of mass parties: The Social Democratic experience 1889–1978', in H. Daalder and P. Mair (eds.), *Western European Party Systems: Continuity and Change*, Beverly Hills, Sage, 1983.

¹⁷ Wellhofer (1979), ibid.

¹⁸ See Brand, *The National Movement in Scotland*, pp. 265–292; Mansbach, *The*

S.N.P.: A revised profile; R. Crawford, 'The S.N.P. 1960–74: An Investigation into its Organisation and Power Structure', Ph.D thesis, University of Glasgow, May 1982; M. V. Kauppi, 'The decline of the S.N.P. 1977–81: Political and organisational factors', *Ethnic and Racial Studies* 5, 3, 1982, pp. 326–348.

19 Mansbach, ibid., p. 189 and Brand, ibid., pp. 283–283; see also V. Hanby, 'The renaissance of the S.N.P.: from eccentric to campaigning crusader', *Sage Electoral Studies Year Book*, Beverly Hills, Sage, 1976, pp. 217–241, and K. Webb, *The Growth of Nationalism in Scotland*, Harmondsworth, Penguin, 1975, p. 144.

20 Mansbach, ibid.

21 Webb's argument that 'between 1962 and 1970, the S.N.P. was transformed into a modern efficient mass political party' is the substance of Crawford's centralist case. Webb, *The Growth of Nationalism in Scotland*, p. 137.

22 Brand, *The National Movement in Scotland*, p. 279.

23 Crawford, *The S.N.P. 1960–74*, p. 192 and pp. 210–212. See also Kauppi, 'The decline of the S.N.P.', p. 167, and C. Harvie, *Scotland and nationalism: Society and Politics, 1707–1977*, London, Allen and Unwin, 1977, p. 252.

24 Crawford, ibid., pp. 257–260.

25 Crawford, ibid., p. 176.

26 Treasurer's report to the National Council, Scottish National Party, Edinburgh, 1 September 1973. See below chapters 3, 4 and 5.

27 W. A. R. Mullin, 'The Scottish National Party', in H. M. Drucker (ed.), *Multi-Party Britain*, London, Macmillan, 1979, pp. 127–129.

28 Miller, *The End of British Politics?*, p. 248.

29 Mullin, in Drucker (ed.), *Multi-Party Britain*, p. 127.

30 Reports of outcomes of business of annual conferences, 1975–79, Scottish National Party, Edinburgh.

31 W. Mishler and A. Mughan, 'Representing the Celtic Fringe: Devolution and legislative Behaviour in Scotland and Wales', *Legislative Studies Quarterly*, 3, 3, 1978, pp. 388–389, Table 2.

32 Mullin, 'The Scottish National Party', p. 129. See also Kauppi, 'The decline of the S.N.P.', pp. 210–211; A. Fusaro, 'Two Faces of British nationalism: The S.N.P. and the P.C. compared', *Polity*, 11, 3, 1979, pp. 362–386 and A. Butt Philip, 'Devolution and regionalism' in C. Cook and J. Ramsden (eds.) *Trends in British Politics since 1945*, London, Macmillan, 1978.

33 Profiles of prospective parliamentary candidates 1970, October 1974 and 1979, Scottish National Party, Edinburgh.

34 These phenomena are by no means unique to the S.N.P. See R. Levy, 'Third Party Decline in the U.K.: The S.N.P. and S.D.P. in Comparative Perspective', *West European Politics*, 11, 3, 1988, pp. 57–74. The same general structural characteristics also apply in the Alliance successor, the Social and Liberal Democrats.

CHAPTER 2

Voters and Strategies

Electoral support for the S.N.P. has been subject to as much inquiry as the origins of nationalism itself. A highly technical and detailed debate at times, at its heart are more general issues concerning the validity of competing theories of voting behaviour. As in the wider U.K. context, the argument revolves around the relative importance 'partisanship' influences, protest and issue voting in determining electoral outcomes. In so far as it addresses the influence of party policies on the voting decision, this debate has profound implications for parties and party strategists alike. In the specific context of the S.N.P.'s growth, it raises the question of whether the party's actions made any significant difference to its performance over the period under review.

Until the mid-1970s, the dominant interpretation of electoral behaviour in the U.K. was based on the partisanship model. In this view, political allegiance and voter bonding resulted from early patterns of socialisation. Support for the major parties was transmitted from one generation to the next in the home and the community, with a tendency for Labour to increase its dominance as the electorate became increasingly homogenised.[1] There was little place for third party growth in this model, although 'protest' voting was a conceivable temporary 'deviation' for Labour or Conservative partisans.

The implications of the partisanship model for party strategy are negative in the extreme. If would-be votes are properly socialised into the political value system of the home and the community, then changes in party policy have no effect on voting behaviour. Voters are simply not predisposed to change a behavioural pattern acquired in their formative years. If this is the case, then there is little incentive for parties either to change their policies, keep the same policies, or indeed have any policies at all. It is not surprising therefore that partisanship models have had relatively little to say about party behaviour, and have tended instead to point out the dissonance between partisan opinion and party policy as a substantiation of their case.[2]

Now, however, the partisanship thesis seems less robust. As Brand *et al.* (1983) note in reference to the U.S. and the U.K., '(l)ater studies of both countries tell a different story'.[3] If nothing else, the electoral reality of the early 1970s demanded a re-assessment of the situation. With the share of the vote going to the major parties falling, the third party vote rising and partisanship evidently weakening, the partisanship model has come under increasing challenge from various issue-voter based models since that period.[4] While there has not been a total rejection of the partisanship model, and the so-called dealignment thesis has itself been questioned, the balance of opinion has shifted decisively towards issue voting. If not for all voters, then the salience of short-run campaign factors, material considerations and other issue positions are generally agreed to have increased in importance for many voters.[5] If this is the case, then party strategy is no longer something which is of importance only to party leaders and activists. It has a direct bearing on the voting decision itself and thus on the level of support a party may expect to enjoy in the opinion polls or at elections.

The debate about the S.N.P. vote and the Scottish electorate has followed these broad contours. Indeed, it has been instrumental in so far as the increasing nationalist vote was an early sign that the prevailing nostrums needed re-examining. Following Budge and Urwin's (1966) pioneering study of Scottish voting behaviour, early investigations of the nationalist electorate tended to focus on the social background characteristics of S.N.P. voters. Finding little or no distinctive sectional or demographic basis, the S.N.P. vote was initially interpreted as a protest vote without further implications. Perhaps best articulated by McLean (1970), the simple protest vote model sought to explain first-time S.N.P. voting in the 1960s. It did not question the underlying bases of political allegiance or suggest that such protest would result in a change in partisanship.

There was disagreement about who these voters actually were however. McLean argued that the S.N.P. vote was predominantly made up of non-partisans, the previously apolitical and new voters rather than Labour or Conservative defectors. If this was the case, then electoral turnout could have been expected to increase as these protestors made their impact felt. The relatively low turnout at the 1970 election thus made this argument difficult to sustain. Kellas (1973), on the other hand, showed that S.N.P. voters in 1968 held a variety of opinions on Scottish issues which were not consonant with S.N.P. policy, and that their attitudes were similar to English 'protestors' who were inconsistent Labour or Conservative supporters.[6] Thus, according to Kellas, the S.N.P. vote was drawn from among weak partisans of the major parties rather than the groups identified by McLean. Bochel and Denver's study (1972) also took issue with McLean, claiming instead that the S.N.P. vote came from those who normally voted Labour, a conclusion later endorsed by Hanby's (1976) local study of S.N.P. voters in the Stirling area.

With the dramatic resurgence of the nationalist vote in 1974, the simple protest vote model was no longer deemed a sufficient explanation in itself, and additions were made to create a 'two stage' model. While voters may have initially voted for the S.N.P. as a protest, this later developed into a more permanent partisan attachment. In the terminology of its proponents such as Jaensch (1976), Hanby (1976), Brand (1978) and Bogdanor (1979), 'national' or 'ethnic' partisanship had either replaced class-based partisanship or added a new dimension to it. Thus, Hanby claimed that 'for many Scottish electors, traditional class loyalties have been replaced by the new catalyst of ethnicity',[7] an assertion based on the proportion of self-proclaimed S.N.P. partisans in the electorate in 1975.

It is, ironically, Baxter-Moore's version of the protest vote thesis (1979), which draws attention to the major defect of the partisanship approach inherent in the two-stage model, viz: the conflation of short term voter preferences and long term party attachments. According to the British Election Survey of October 1974, 67·2% of S.N.P. voters identified themselves with the party. Baxter-Moore cautions 'that there may well be an over-reporting of identification with the S.N.P. and an under-reporting of long-term attachments with other parties'.[8] As Miller (1981) points out, there is a tendency among British voters to identify with the parties they last voted for whether they have a long term attachment to them or not. While voters may be berated for failing to distinguish between long and short term allegiances, this affixes blame to the singers rather than the political scientist songwriters. If this is the case, then it does throw some doubt on the usefulness of the partisanship concept as a predictor of voting behaviour.

Rejecting the idea of a rapid rise in S.N.P. partisanship in the early 1970s does not necessarily invalidate the argument that a more general national or ethnic partisanship had been mobilised in the form of S.N.P. support however. This subtle but important distinction between national/ethnic consciousness and S.N.P. partisanship allows for the growth of S.N.P. support within the overall framework of the partisanship model. While national consciousness make S.N.P. partisanship possible, it does not make it inevitable. Thus, Brand (1978) argues for a protest explanation plus 'those theories which attribute the situation to the rise of national consciousness in Scotland, which in turn led to a demand for national self determination'.[9]

The protest vote model can explain why Scots turned away from the old parties, but it cannot explain why they turned to nationalism according to Brand. Using data from one study conducted in Glasgow, Brand shows that most S.N.P. voters supported the party because they thought it was 'good for Scotland' rather than because they agreed with its policies, a position also taken by Kellas (1973, 1976) and Baxter-Moore (1979). However, as Brand himself points out, national awareness is long-standing and perennial, and the question ineviatably arises as to why it was not politicised before. Given that 'issue' voting is ruled out, protest is an essential component if this theory of S.N.P. voting is to work.

It is for this reason and because of his reservations about the supposed partisanship of S.N.P. voters, that Baxter-Moore makes such a determined effort to reconstruct the protest vote model. He identifies three types of protest voters, viz: the short term protestor who votes against his own party once but remains basically committed to it, the protest movement supporter who rejects the existing party system rather than one particular party and expresses support for an anti-system movement or party, and finally, the tactical voter who supports his second choice party in order to displace the incumbent party which he dislikes most. Taken together, Baxter-Moore argues that these elements of protest voting constituted up to half the S.N.P. vote in 1974.

If this is the case, the 1974 elections have to be considered 'deviant' cases, after which short term and tactical voters reverted to their 'normal' allegiances, and protest movement voters lost faith. This argument thus separates the protestors from the partisans in such a way as to decouple completely the two-stage model outlined earlier. According to Baxter-Moore, S.N.P. partisanship grew steadily, independently of protest voting, with the voters that were left in 1979 constituting the real S.N.P. partisans. The only problem is that the long term growth in S.N.P. partisanship remains unexplained. It clearly has nothing to do with short term influences, which are specifically rejected by Baxter-Moore.

The alternative is to reject the partisanship and protest models in favour of some kind of issue vote thesis. The case for this interpretation is most cogently argued by Miller et al. (1980) and

Miller (1981). After confirming the S.N.P.'s lack of any significant sectional base among Scottish voters, Miller argues that S.N.P. voters in 1974 were characterised by their distinct concern for Scottish issues rather than any distinctly 'Scottish' characteristics they did or did not share. In fact, the social background characteristics of S.N.P. voters as measured in terms of religion, house tenure, class identification, unskilled and self employment, and family size, deviated away from the Scottish mean and towards the southern English mean. Nevertheless, these voters were 'Superscots' in terms of their attitudes, principally towards economic expectations and perceptions, policy salience and policy positions, and party evaluation, perceptions and like.[10]

In common with findings on Liberal voters in England, Miller found that S.N.P. voters identified with the party's issue positions rather than with the party as such, and preferred the party to any other on the two specifically Scottish issues of oil and devolution. However, it was not the case that the S.N.P. simply mobilised pro-devolutionary sentiment and turned it into votes. This only happened where pro-devolutionary attitudes combined with balanced attitudes towards the Labour and Conservative parties in areas where the S.N.P. was already strong, and as a result of certain fortuitous events which focused attention on these issues – the oil crisis and the general election campaigns of 1974, for example.

This begs the question of how Miller arrives at the conclusion that the attitudes to devolution were fundamental to everything else. On the surface, there is nothing to prevent a resurrection of the protest vote model, albeit a partially issue driven one, especially when the low priority accorded to devolution by voters is taken into account (Kellas (1976)). Miller's methodology in fact takes pains to try to isolate the major influences and to show the manner in which they combine precisely for this reason. Thus, although his data do show that 'pro-Scottish' attitudes on oil and devolution and distrust of the major parties were highly predictive of S.N.P. voting, devolution attitudes on their own had the strongest single influence.

As the S.N.P. is in favour of independence rather than devolution, this may seem somewhat paradoxical and lend support to the partisanship and protest vote models. Brand et al. argue that '(i)f electors voted for the Nationalists because they agreed with their policy of independence for Scotland, this would be real issue voting', and they attribute only about a quarter of the S.N.P. vote in 1974 and 1979 to usse voters of this kind.[11]

There are a number of possible explanations for this apparent inconsistency. First, it could be argued that voters responded to their own perceptions rather than any accurate perception of party policy. Miller found that practically all voters (95%) thought that the S.N.P. was very much in favour of devolution, a far higher percentage than that achieved by any other party.[12] Even among those in favour of independence, presumably mostly S.N.P. voters, 97% supported devolution. Miller concludes therefore that pro-devolution and pro-independence attitudes were not seen as either separate or contradictory by voters 'as they could so reasonably have been'.[13] There was no dissonance between S.N.P. policy and the attitudes of S.N.P. voters because none was perceived by voters at the time. Perverse it may be, but it does support the issue vote thesis nevertheless.

It may have been the case however, that S.N.P. voters who favoured devolution were still issue voters because they judged the S.N.P. 'as the only party seriously committed to this end'.[14] According to Brand et al., there was a correlation between pro-devolutionary sentiment and S.N.P. voting in 1974, but in 1979, it was equally correlated with Labour voting, i.e. when Labour was also claiming to be the party of devolution. In this case, voters responded 'rationally' to changes in party policy. As Brand et al. conclude, while 'the majority of those who voted for the S.N.P. did indeed support devolution rather than independence . . . a Nationalist vote cannot automatically be regarded as a vote upon the issue'.[15]

In this case, it may be asked why such voters did not switch to the Liberal Party in 1974 rather than the S.N.P. If it was simply a question of unsullied issue voting, then an upsurge in the Liberal vote in Scotland could have been expected, given that party's long-standing commitment to 'Home Rule', and the apparently close 'fit' between voter attitudes and Liberal Party policy. Instead, it was the S.N.P., officially committed to independence and not devolution, which benefited. While voters' misperceptions about S.N.P. policy may have been 'genuine' (which would maintain the integrity of the issue vote model), it can also be argued that voters who were predisposed to vote Nationalist simply constructed the policy reality which suited their inclinations. Just as partisanship may have been overstated, so issue voting may have been over-reported. As Brand et al. point out, voters may consider it more 'respectable' to justify their actions by reference to issues than any other less 'rational' reason.

Whatever else, this evidence does suggest that the S.N.P. could still be accommodated within the safe parameters of the emerging devolution debate as far as the electorate was concerned. If the party did indeed perceive the situation accurately, then in Downsian terms, it could have been expected to adopt a deliberately ambiguous strategy in order to pass off independence as some form of 'super devolution'. On the other hand, the danger of such a strategy was that the electorate would in time come to see devolution as simply a variant of independence. This was perhaps the achievement of the 'No' forces during the 1979 referendum campaign, aided inadvertently by the Nationalists themselves.

Moreover, if devolution and independence remained one and the same for voters in 1974, this was not the case with devolution and the Scotland Act in 1979. Miller shows that while party differences reached over 50% on the Act by the day of the referendum, they reached only 20% on devolution per se. The Scottish electorate remained decisively pro-devolutionist while at the same time 'rejecting' the Scotland Act on the party grounds.[16] This does undermine Miller's thesis somewhat. If pro-devolution attitudes could not accurately predict support for real devolution, what use could they be on their own in predicting S.N.P. support? It would seem that attitudes to devolution were overlain by partisan loyalties which, in the circumstances of March 1979, proved to be very influential. There have to be other supporting factors as Miller himself argues.

Some of these were issue based, but one cannot escape the fact that the other – distrust of the major parties – was protest based. The average S.N.P. voter in 1974 was an amalgam. On the issue side, these voters played down the importance of British issues generally, while stressing the importance of Scottish issues. In addition to devolution, they showed distinctive attitudes towards North Sea ('Scottish') oil as Miller *et al.* (1980) confirm. S.N.P. voters were most distinctive in their critical attitude towards government policy, their desire for a slow-down in the rate of extraction, their optimism over Scotland's economic prospects and their desire for a strong Scottish bias in the apportionment of the oil revenues. Attitudes towards oil-related issues showed an even greater fluctuation than attitidues to devolution over the 1974–79 period, with all voters moving away from a pro-Scottish view towards a pro-British view in varying degrees.[17]

In any case, it would be a mistake to over-estimate the general support for the S.N.P.'s stated position on oil, or of the concern felt for the issue per se. The S.N.P. had certainly established itself as the most pro-Scottish party on oil by a huge margin in 1974, but only a small minority of voters supported an all-for-Scotland policy. Even in 1974, when support for a pro-Scottish oil was at its height, S.N.P. voters only opted for the two strongest positions by the narrowest of margins, and the percentage favouring the strongest pro-Scottish policy was practically the same as those favouring the strongest pro-British policy (i.e. 16% and 15% respectively).[18]

Given the dissonance between voter opinion and S.N.P. policy on oil that existed even in 1974, it is hardly surprising that the party lost its lead in popularity on the issue in the less favourable climate of 1979. Although voters thought all parties were more pro-British on oil by 1979, the S.N.P. was so strongly associated with the pro-Scottish position that there was a 'massive drop' in its popularity on the issue according to Miller *et al.*[19]

How important then were oil attitudes as a determinant of S.N.P. voting? A pure oil driven model of S.N.P. support is rejected by Miller *et al.* on the grounds that during the period when the oil discoveries were made (1970–74), there was no increase in support for devolution or independence. Thus, pro-Scots oil attitudes did not result in any change in opinion on the wider constitutional question. This is a rather questionable assumption because there are no data measuring attitudes on oil or devolution for the period between 1970 and February 1974. It simply cannot be said with any certainty what opinions Scots voters held on either issue therefore. Indeed, it would not be unreasonable to argue on the basis of Miller's own observations, that there was an upsurge of 'pro-Scots' opinions on these issues when the Kilbrandon Commission report was published in 1973, or when the S.N.P. launched the 'It's Scotland's Oil' campaign in 1972 for example. The truth is that nobody knows. Notwithstanding this caveat, Miller *et al.* return to an interactive issue vote model, in which oil attitudes played an important but subsidiary role to devolution attitudes in determining S.N.P. voting in 1974 and 1979.[20]

However, in the light of the either balanced trust in, or total distrust of the major U.K. parties typically shown by S.N.P. voters in 1974, it is difficult to see how the protest vote model can be rejected, at least for some S.N.P. voters. Indeed, there is no need to do so, as the protest thesis does not have to be a corollary of the partisanship model. Having said that, it would seem quite likely that a decline in partisanship might precede protest, which itself might precede pro-Scots attitudes on oil and devolution. To extend Miller *et al.*'s own chain, instead of

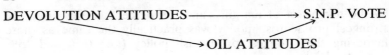

DEVOLUTION ATTITUDES ──────────────→ S.N.P. VOTE

──────→ OIL ATTITUDES

we have

WEAKENED → PROTEST → DEVOLUTION → S.N.P. VOTE
PARTISANSHIP   ATTITUDES

OIL ATTITUDES

In the final analysis, it simply cannot be proven that the S.N.P. vote was really 'caused' by voter issue attitudes, as it cannot be proven that pro-Scottish attitudes on either oil or devolution were anterior to any predisposition to vote Nationalist. The fact that 65% of Miller's Scottish sample in 1974 claimed that they liked the party – a far higher percentage than English respondents liked any British party – and an overwhelming majority thought that the S.N.P. had been good for Scotland seem to suggest a basic goodwill towards the S.N.P. irrespective of its policies.[21] Issue positions can be constructed as *ex post facto* rationalisations for something voters were going to do anyway on the grounds of protest or sentiment.

In contrast to the studies made in the mid-1970s, the case for ethnic partisanship is not well-supported by the evidence presented by Brand *et al.* (1983). They found that national identification had not replaced class identification as the most salient political cleavage in Scotland, and concluded that 'there is certainly little evidence from the sense of Scottish nationality or from partisanship that a new cleavage structure has appeared. Class, though diminished in importance, still seems to have more force than nationality, and the partisanship of the older parties is stronger than that of the S.N.P.'[22]

Nevertheless, the decline in class partisanship and the increasing salience of political issues led Brand *et al.* to argue for a combination of explanations which is supportive of the protest thesis. In fact, two of their main contentions directly support the Baxter-Moore protest model outlined earlier. They found that many Labour and Conservative identifiers had in fact voted tactically for the S.N.P. in 1974 and 1979 as a form of protest against local incumbents belonging to their least liked party. Citing Pinard's (1971) evidence on protest voting and one party dominance in Quebec, they suggest that this form of protest is particularly likely in Scottish constituences displaying the same characteristics. Such circumstances, in their view, allowed 'the opening of a cleavage on Scottish–English lines'.[23] While this is hardly consistent with the general picture of class partisanship which they present, it suggests a limited breakdown of this form of allegiance in some places.

This latter idea is particularly interesting, as a new cleavage line is not a necessary consequence of one party dominance. Pinard's study of Social Credit is supportive of a pure protest thesis in so far as the Créditiste vote underwent a spectacular rise and an equally spectacular fall without any new cleavage appearing. What was its origin in the Scottish case then? The answer is probably to be found in the peculiar form of class partisanship in Scotland. The earlier work by Miller *et al.* (1980) found that Labour and Conservative partisans in Scotland took a consistently 'pro-Scots' view of their parties' positions, irrespective of these parties' actual positions. 'Class' partisanship in Scotland does not preclude an ethnic coating which may be influential under certain circumstances, such as protest or tactical voting. Indeed, if the trappings of class partisanship are cast aside either partially or completely, the layer of ethnicity which adhered to it may still be retained and assume a much greater significance.

Also supportive of the protest vote thesis, Brand *et al.* found that the abandonment of the S.N.P. by significant numbers of voters in 1979 was not accompanied by a rise in major party identification. This indicated continuing disillusion with the party system. Using Smelser's (1963) well-known framework of collective action, Brand *et al.* argue that the political system was under evident strain from at least the mid-1960s, and that weakening partisanship was merely one manifestation of it. Thus, their conclusion that 'policy preference was influential in determining partisanship' rather than the other way round has to be seen in this context.[24] If voters were being prised away from their traditional loyalties and towards a consideration of the issues, it was within a framework of protest which could take on an 'ethnic' form. This conclusion is supported by Studley and McAllister's (1988) recent study on nationalism and post-industrial values, which suggests that nationalist protest is one incarnation of the new value agenda which animates an increasingly large proportion of the electorate.

S.N.P. Strategy – An Overview

For whatever reasons, the early 1970s were a window of opportunity for the S.N.P. Scottish voters were amenable as never before to the issue cues of the Nationalists on 'Scottish' matters. The extent to which the S.N.P. was able to take advantage of this situation, or indeed actually create it, is the subject matter of the following chapters. Our purpose here is to elaborate the more general context of the party's policy development and campaigning strategies.

The first question concerns the party's general ability to adapt its existing policies and develop new ones. In line with Downs's assumptions concerning party rationality, McAllister's study of nationalist parties in the U.K. (1980), suggests that this is very important. According to McAllister, a successful electoral strategy required the development of a 'programmatic' orientation, based on a recognition of the need for negotiation and compromise, at the expense of any 'overriding goals' of the parties concerned. As we have argued, such adaptation may be difficult for organisational reasons. In this case, did the S.N.P. seek to modify its long term objectives in the interests of electoral expediency, or did it merely husband its resources while steadfastly maintaining its fundamental aim to the exclusion of all else? Alternatively, was the party developing intermediate policies?

Irrespective of whether it modified its long term aim or not, the party had become quite effective at targetting its resources by 1974. According to Miller's analysis of the S.N.P. vote in 1974 and patterns of campaign expenditure and previous candidature, the party performed best in the 19 constituencies where it had done well in 1970 or at a by-election. Of the 20 seats that the party spent most in, no fewer than 14 of them were in this group. Conversely, of the 19 seats in which the party spent least, 18 were in Glasgow and its environs, an area of relatively poor performance for the party, and one incidentally, where many of the seats were dominated by a single party (Labour).[25] Thus, Miller concludes that the S.N.P.'s campaign of February 1974 was directed at rural Scotland and the seats in which it had already done well, and was designed to take maximum advantage of a spatially uneven distribution of support.

As for policy, McAllister takes the view that U.K. ethno-nationalist parties generally have developed intermediate range policies as a result of their increasingly electoral orientation.[26] McAllister's general argument concerning the fact of the S.N.P.'s transformation is supported by Webb (1977), Mullin (1979) and Miller (1981). They all claim that the party has shown great flexibility on the traditional class-based issues of British politics. Indeed, what is significant is not the flexibility, but the fact that the S.N.P. has seen fit to address these issues at all. It has not simply concentrated on exclusively 'Scottish' issues. In an analysis of the S.N.P.'s election manifesto for October 1974, Birch (1977) found that no less than 56% of the content was devoted to general domestic policies, with only 20% and 14% devoted respectively to independence and oil and energy.[27]

This is almost certainly something of a recent phenomenon in the S.N.P.'s case. Webb (1977) argues that the party did not have any short range policies until the mid-1960s, and indeed the mechanisms to devise them did not exist until the Party's National Assembly set up the twenty or so policy committees in 1969, which even then, had only a fitful existence until the successes of 1974. However, this broadening of the policy agenda may not have produced many benefits for the party. In contrast to McAllister's hypothesis, Brand *et al.* (1983) argue that the voters' perception of the S.N.P.'s transformation from a movement to a party was one of the reasons for its loss of support in 1979. The development of new policies coincided with what many have seen as an ideological split between traditionalists and pragmatists, as the older leaders were displaced in the organisational expansion of the 1960s by those who were not primarily motivated by elemental nationalism.[28] While this may have been acceptable as a growing pain, its persistence in the party's more mature phases of development has been a profoundly negative influence. Hostility to 'policy making' is a constant fact of life in the S.N.P. Only its intensity varies.

Secondly, the party was only popular during the 1970s on the distinctively Scottish issues of oil and devolution, where it was perceived to have clearcut positions. Somewhat ironically in the light of the current policy of 'Independence within the EC', Webb (1977) argues that it also had a clearcut policy of opposition to the European Community, but efforts that were made to diversify the party's policy image were largely wasted as nobody paid any attention to them. Thus, success or failure hinged on the ability to manage these two interrelated issues, and the acid test of the party's commitment to modify and develop its policies in tune with electoral preferences must be made on its strategy on these issues.

As we have seen, oil and devolution were linked issues for the Scottish electorate – as indeed they were for the S.N.P. – and different attitudes towards them made voters, in Miller's words, 'more or less responsive to the campaigning appeals of the S.N.P.'[29] They presented very different strategic problems for the party however. North Sea oil was an ideal sectional issue for the S.N.P., and has been frequently described as a capaiging gift for the party. As Furnivall (1939) and Rabushka and Shepsle (1972) have argued, the rational strategy for ethnic political producers such as the S.N.P. to pursue is to seek out and exploit sectional differences in the 'collective' goods market. By seeking to reserve the benefits of a 'national' resource exclusively for one ethnic segment, they can expect to raise their office holding prospects within that segment. North Sea oil was just such an issue for the S.N.P., and thus almost a liability for the British parties in Scotland. Neither the Labour nor Conservative parties, as British parties, could really promise any 'exclusive' benefit to Scotland without risking damage to their popularity elsewhere. Neither rushed in to capitalise on the implications of the discoveries for Scotland, and they both sought to play down the extent of the reserves and the benefits from them in the initial phases. Indeed, it was difficult to find a Labour response at all during the early period of the Conservative government of 1970–74 when the first discoveries were being made.

When external circumstances forced the issue onto the political agenda, control of the oil was cast by the major parties as an ideological issue on the private versus public dimension, and not a sectional issue. They were both agreed that the oil was British. The S.N.P. sought to redefine the terms of the debate and arguably succeeded at doing so in Scotland. Even if voters arrived at 'pro-Scots' positions independently, the S.N.P. was able to occupy the most popular position on the issue for much of the 1970s, and dictated when and how oil was salient as a political issue for at least two years. Thus, North Sea oil presented one of those rare instances of a new and particularly favourable issue for a third party which could be used as vehicle for significant growth.

The question of devolved government for Scotland was far more problematic for the S.N.P., as it impinged on the party's central long term aim of sovereignty, and exposed the ideological division in the party referred to already. Complete independence for Scotland had enjoyed only minority support (around 20%), within the Scottish electorate since at least 1964,[30] and was strongly identified with the S.N.P. Thus, barring any major shift in public opinion on this issue, the party had a number of choices. It could stick to its goal to the exclusion of any further growth of electoral support, or perhaps modify its goal in the direction of support for some kind of 'home rule' – at least in the short term – and hope to extend its electoral base. The problem was that it had always rejected such intermediate policies in the past. They were not popular within the party, either at conference or among many of the leaders. Alternatively, it could pursue a classic Downsian strategy of ambiguity, hoping that the electorate would either come to view that independence was just another variant of acceptable devolution, or that the party was not really serious about independence anyway.

In contrast to the oil issue, the S.N.P. was unable to dictate the terms of political debate to its competitors. It could not demonstrate the same evident sectional advantages for independence as it could on the oil issue. Nor did it succeed in linking these two. In the context of the materialistic rather than cultural orientation of voters to the constitutional issue, such a deficiency was fatal. Indeed, given the deeply held opinions about independence, the party will probably always have difficulties in convincing many voters about the viability of such a radical project, no matter how strong its case.

In the context of its own hesitancy about devolution, the S.N.P. found itself entering the political arena on terms not of its own making. Although it would have been difficult for the S.N.P. to take a positive lead, advocate the case for devolved government in Scotland within a U.K. framework and simultaneously drop its commitment to independence as a realistic goal, this was essentially what was required. It was not an impossible task. The Labour government had only very reluctantly entered the field as the party of devolution, and was constantly assailed by many of its backbench supporters for doing so. There was a strategic opportunity for the S.N.P. to shift its ground, and it almost succeeded in doing so. To the relief of party traditionalists and competitor parties alike, it did not.

These two issues thus provide contrasting perspectives from which to view the behaviour of the S.N.P., and in particular the interaction of the organisational processes typical of an organisation of this type outlined in chapter 1. The consequences of these processes will be reviewed in the next three chapters.

Notes

[1] See, for example, D. Butler and D. Stokes, *Political Change in Britain*, 2nd college edn, New York, St Martins Press, 1976, and P. Pulzer *Political Representation and Elections in Britain*, 2nd edn, London, Allen and Unwin, 1972.

[2] Butler and Stokes, ibid., p. 216. For a confirmation of the partisanship model from a former critic, see M. Harrop, 'Beliefs, Feelings and Votes: The British Case', *British Journal of Political Science*, 7, 3, 1977, p. 319.

[3] J. Brand, D. McLean and W. Miller, 'The Birth and Death of a Three Party System; Scotland in the Seventies', *British Journal of Political Science*, 13, 1983, p. 464.

[4] See especially the famous 1977 article on dealignment by Ivor Crewe and his colleagues. I. Crewe, B. Sarlvik and J. Alt, 'Partisan Dealignment in Britain 1964–74', *British Journal of Political Science*, 7, 4, 1977, pp. 129–190.

[5] See especially R. Rose and I. McAllister, *Voters Begin to Choose*, London, Sage, 1986, and H. Himmelweit, P. Humphreys and M. Jaeger, *How Voters Decide; A longitudinal study of political attitudes and voting extending over fifteen years*, Milton Keynes, Open University Press, 1985.

[6] J. Kellas, *The Scottish Political System*, Cambridge, Cambridge University Press, 1973, p. 139.

[7] V. Hanby, 'Current Scottish Nationalism', in R. Parsler (ed.), *Capitalism, Class and Politics in Scotland*, Gower, Farnborough, 1980, p. 114.

[8] N. Baxter-Moore, 'The Rise and Fall of the S.N.P.: Revisited', paper delivered to the European Politics Workshop, Ontario, 1979, p. 30.

[9] J. Brand, *The National Movement in Scotland*, London, Routledge, 1978, p. 293.

[10] W. L. Miller, *The End of British Politics? Scots and English Political Behaviour in the Seventies*, Oxford, Clarendon, 1981, p. 152.

[11] Brand *et al.*, *Birth and Death of a Three Party System*, pp. 465 and 467.

[12] Miller, *The End of British Politics?*, p. 122. The S.N.P.'s position on devolution was by no means clear at this time; see ch. 4 below.

[13] Ibid., p. 107.

[14] Brand *et al.*, *Birth and Death of a Three Party System*, p. 468.

[15] Ibid., p. 472.

[16] Miller, *The End of British Politics?*, p. 251. In the referendum, S.N.P. voters were by far the most consistent in favouring devolution and actually voting for it.

[17] See Miller's 'oil benefit index', ibid., Table 15, p. 68.

[18] W. Miller, J. Brand and M. Jordan, *Oil and the Scottish Voter, 1974–79*, London, Social Science Research Council, 1980, p. 69. The figures relate only to 1979 when just 6% of the sample preferred an 'all for Scotland' policy. A Scotsman/ORC poll of October 1975 showed only a 10% level of support for this position; *The Scotsman*, 14 October 1975.

[19] Miller *et al.*, *Oil and the Scottish Voter*, p. 69.

[20] Ibid., pp. 80–87.

[21] Miller, *The End of British Politics?*, pp. 91–92.

[22] Brand *et al.*, *Birth and Death of a Three Party System*, p. 478.

[23] Ibid., p. 481.

[24] Ibid., p. 483.

[25] Miller, *The End of British Politics?*, pp. 200–210.

[26] I. McAllister, *Party Organisation and Minority Nationalism: A Comparative Study in the U.K.*, Glasgow, Centre for the Study of Public Policy, 1980.

[27] A. Birch, *Political Integration and Disintegration in the British Isles*, London, Allen and Unwin, 1979, p. 113.

[28] See C. Harvie, *Scotland and Nationalism: Scottish Society and Politics 1707–1977*, London, Allen and Unwin, 1977, p. 241; K. Webb, *The Growth of Nationalism in Scotland*, Harmondsworth, Penguin, pp. 139–144; M. Kauppi, 'The Decline of the S.N.P. 1977–81; Political and Organisational Factors', *Ethnic and Racial Studies*, 5, 3, 1982, p. 173; McAllister, *Party Organisation and Minority Nationalism*, p. 28.

[29] Miller *et al.*, *Oil and the Scottish Voter*, p. 77.

[30] Miller, *The End of British Politics?*, pp. 99–101.

CHAPTER 3

Campaigning for Growth: Oil-fired Nationalism

In the annals of modern Scottish nationalism, there is one issue other than independence with which the S.N.P. is readily identified: 'Scotland's oil'. The party's use of the discovery and exploitation of the U.K.'s North Sea oil reserves as a political issue is generally regarded as a great success. Most agree that the 'It's Scotland's Oil' campaign launched in 1972 was responsible for a renewed bout of organisational growth and, perhaps more importantly, the party's maturation into a flexible and pragmatic electoral machine unencumbered by dogma.[1]

This latter development was critical, for it marked off the party's achievements in the 1970s from the earlier period of organisational expansion in the 1960s. The Hamilton by-election of 1967 and the successes in local elections in 1968 had proved that the party was capable of rapid short-term growth, but subsequent events showed that it was capable of equally rapid decline. Capitalising on feelings of Scottish identity and protest voting against the major parties were insufficient in themselves to sustain a nationalist upswing into the 1970 election. While these results were a dramatic improvement over the 1966 performance, they nevertheless represented a steep decline from those achieved at the local elections in 1968. To make matters worse, figures for party membership showed that serious organisational shrinkage was in progress too.[2]

The oil campaign attempted to break this brush-fire cycle. Even if it was not the party's first attempt, the campaign certainly represented the first serious effort to diversify its campaigning appeal beyond the constitutional question. By 1974, the S.N.P. had managed to establish itself as the most pro-Scottish party on oil. According to one survey, 82% of Scottish voters thought that the S.N.P. wanted all the benefits for Scotland and total Scottish control.[3] Although these policies were not unreservedly endorsed

by public opinion, they were far more popular than those on offer
from the other parties. The economic case for independence could
no longer be simply ignored. The major parties were forced to
take the S.N.P.'s economic arguments seriously for the first time.
Indeed, the lingering effect of these arguments is now evident in
the Labour Party's own proposals for a Scottish Assembly.

North sea oil opened up a new area of debate in which the
S.N.P. could participate to great advantage compared to the British
parties. Despite some initial misgivings about using the issue, the
party put forward specific proposals concerning rates of extraction,
taxation, offshore supplies, state intervention and oil-funded
projects, while at the same time making the more general case for
independence. The oil issue could be made general or specific,
Scottish or British, constitutional or economic as required. The
party's credibility was generally buttressed by its consistently
accurate forecasts concerning the extent of the oil reserves, rates
of extraction, and the likely revenues that would accrue to the
government. Paradoxically, its own campaigning efforts were
supplemented by the actions of its competitors. Given the critical
importance attached to North Sea oil for the British economy after
the oil 'shock' of October 1973 by the British parties, the issue
became in Miller's words, a 'usefully multifaceted' one for the
S.N.P.[4]

It would have been surprising therefore if the S.N.P. had not
exploited the oil issue. Multifaceted or not, however, the oil issue
did not produce anything like a consistent approach from the
party. The organisational behaviour of the S.N.P. on the oil issue
was in fact complex, hesitant and often contradictory. While the
party did possess 'market oriented' campaigning capabilities to
some degree at the beginning of the 1970s, it neither had them in
abundance nor did it give them consistent prominence within the
decision-making process. This does not mean that the caricature of
the S.N.P. as a decentralised mass party, in which the membership
constrained the leaders to modify vote winning policies in favour
of long term ideological goals is accurate, and that the centralist
model is inaccurate. On the contrary, the development of the
oil policy tends to support the latter thesis – but not without
modification. The party's involvement with the oil issue was more
complex and incremental than it might have been if high growth
strategies had been completely in command. The constraining
forces did not fundamentally spring from the party's mass membership however.

So, while 'It's Scotland's Oil' may be the best example to date
of the S.N.P.'s attempts to develop short to medium range 'pre-

independence' policies, the effectiveness of the campaign was dissipated before its full potential could be realised. In analysing the progress of the oil issue from the discovery stage through the intensive campaigning stages to eclipse and decline, we will show how these constraints affected party strategy, and from what sources they originated.

Discovering the oil issue

The origin of the S.N.P.'s oil campaign can be traced back fairly precisely to October 1970. The September meeting of the S.N.P's National Council had applied itself to developing a four year strategy for growth and recruitment, and had simply resolved to commit the party to a long march towards national independence. There seemed to be little alternative but to reaffirm the party's basic goal. The idea of an electoral pact with the Liberals had been recirculated in the autumn, but had come to nothing. The only continuing campaign was the party's opposition to British membership of the E.E.C. There was no hint that offshore oil was to play any role in the party's plans.

In the week before the party's annual conference assembled in October, British Petroleum (B.P.) had announced that it was 'hopeful' of making the first-ever commercial oil strike in British waters in an exploration block 110 miles north east of Aberdeen, and on 22 October, front page coverage was given to the arrival on the Scottish mainland of the first oil from what was to become the giant 'Forties' oil and gas field.[5] It was at this time that the idea of using the nascent oil issue as a propaganda weapon occurred to at least some individuals in the party leadership. Reports of a letter sent to the Secretary of State for Scotland by Gordon Wilson, the S.N.P.'s national secretary, appeared in the press on the same day. The letter requested that all rents and royalties from the North Sea be put into a separate Scottish account and be used solely for the benefit of Scotland, and that in addition, all servicing facilities for the North Sea operations be based in Aberdeen rather than Newcastle.

On the strength of this initiative, Gordon Wilson, one of the architects of the party's organisational reforms in the 1960s, started to build a small team centred on the party's research department. This devised, controlled and drove forward the party's strategy in the initial phases. Thus, although the party's official campaign was some two years away, the organisational groundwork had already begun. The necessary catalyst arguably came from outside however, in the form of the Organisation of Petroleum Exporting Countries (O.P.E.C.) – and not for the last time either. At the

February meeting of O.P.E.C. held in Teheran, it was decided to impose a unilateral price rise in the prevailing seller's market for crude where demand was outstripping supply internationally at the rate of half a million barrels per day. At the same time, the pace of exploration and development in the North Sea was accelerating, so that by the summer an 'oil rush' was in progress, and scarcely a day passed in the autumn without some reportage of these developments in the Scottish press.

The S.N.P.'s research department began to take a serious interest in this activity early in 1971. It started to gather data on the likely scale of the reserves, possible rates of extraction, taxation policy and likely revenues, economic spinoffs and the legal basis of a Scottish claim to the resources. The party leadership chose to disseminate this information to the wider sections of the party initially through the medium of the National Council. Judging by the response, there seemed to be no fundamental objection to using the oil issue as a component of the party's campaigning strategy. In May, the party's annual conference passed a resolution from the Maxwellton and Forfar branches affirming Scotland's right to ownership of 'all fuels found off the Scottish coast', and in June the National Council endorsed a resolution drawing attention to the 'assets of incalculable value being exploited by the oil companies off our shores and from which only a self-governing Scotland can benefit'.[6]

Convinced supporters of an oil campaign thus seemed to be under no pressure from party members to modify their views. From the evidence, it appeared that an oil campaign would be popular within the party. Yet events were to show that there was not unreserved endorsement for such a strategy. A limited opportunity to test public reaction presented itself when a parliamentary by-election was called for the Stirling and East Falkirk constituency for September. Interestingly, the S.N.P. candidate chose not to make oil the predominant theme of his campaign until the last few days of the hustings. At this stage, the party candidate and veteran president of the party, Dr Robert McIntyre, issued the text of a letter that he had sent to the Prime Minister and the Leader of the Opposition, in which he accused both major parties of suppressing the extent of the oil wealth, as it would finally destroy the argument that Scotland had insufficient resources 'for prosperity'.[7]

This was not a particularly original theme as it only repeated a view which had already appeared in the press in the summer. It gave the impression that the party had picked up the issue in an ad hoc fashion, despite the behind-the-scenes research and preparation which had in fact been taking place. This suggests that the issue may have been more internally divisive than appeared to be the case on the surface, as Miller (1981) argues it was all along.[8] The 'traditionalists' in the leadership, of whom Dr McIntyre was perhaps the most prominent representative, might have been dubious about an oil campaign on the grounds that it diverted attention from the party's central goal of independence.

Such opposition was weakened by the by-election result. Party leaders seemed to have been convinced that the oil factor had made a positive contribution to the size of the S.N.P. vote. The party Chairman, William Wolfe, immediately appointed Dr McIntyre as the party's official spokesman on oil, and no time was wasted in identifying weaknesses in the campaigning machinery, which had been split between the campaigns department and the publicity committee. Following an emergency resolution to the National Council in September, the two bodies were merged, so bringing together all those individuals who were most involved in the oil campaign. Furthermore, a pilot scheme for the main campaign was announced by Dr McIntyre on 7 October, which consisted of a series of meetings designed to publicise the extent of the reserves and raise public awareness.[9]

The pro-oil faction was strengthened when the government published revised estimates of peak annual production on the day after the Stirling by-election. The highest estimate hitherto had been 50 million tons, but on September 17, the government announced that an output of 150 million tons per annum was possible by 1980. Whether or not Scottish Office ministers had these estimates before 17 September, the suspicion was aroused that the figures had been concealed until after the by-election so as to minimise their political impact. It appeared that ministers were already aware of the value of oil as a propaganda weapon for the Nationalists. The S.N.P. charge that the major parties were holding back on the extent of the reserves seemed to be confirmed.

Yet the party was still tentative in its approach. The next major S.N.P. initiative came in a letter to the Prime Minister released to the press on the 22 November which sought the creation of a 'Scottish oil board' to finance on-shore and industrial development from oil revenues. Designed ostensibly to create 200,000 jobs, these proposals appeared some two weeks after a similar idea had been put forward by the Scottish Liberal Party. Thus, although the Nationalists were claiming increases in membership from 'their' campaign, they were not the only party in Scotland trying to capitalise on the issue, nor had they yet made it exclusively their own. The oil campaigners within party had moved quite cautiously during 1971, and had reacted to the issue in an incremental way, taking small initiatives and adjusting organisational resources on the basis of these limited successes.

Issue prioritisation

A fundamental change was in progress, however. By the end of the year the party leadership was giving the issue the highest priority. In his report to the December meeting of the National Council, the party chairman stated that oil 'should be the most important element in our propaganda for a long time to come. With skilful propagation, it could be the greatest emotional-economic issue in Scotland between now and the next election'.[10] Every party member was urged to inform himself about the implications of the oil discoveries for a self-governing Scotland, and the vice-chairman for publicity was instructed to produce a leaflet and other material.

This upgrading coincided with the growing belief that the other parties were vulnerable on the issue, a perception which was reflected in some sections of the Scottish media. On 30 December, the research department released details of its first 'briefing document' on oil, which included estimates of revenues and jobs based on an annual production figure of 150 million tons. According to The Scotsman, these estimates were 'the latest chapter of the voluminous homework the S.N.P. have (sic) been doing on North Sea oil'[11]. While the other parties did have policies on North Sea oil to a greater or lesser extent (the government, for example, had a well-established policy of licensing and encouraging exploration by the oil companies, and Labour conversely favoured more state control), neither of the main parties had a specifically pro-Scottish policy. The object of the S.N.P.'s endeavours was precisely to develop one.

This was by no means a no- or even low-cost exercise, however. As the party began to divert more of its resources into planning an oil campaign, so signs of both logistical strain and internal debate began to emerge. There was evidence of the former in the party chairman's report to the meeting of the National Council held in March 1972 where it was noted that party finances were being severely drained by the various trips abroad connected with oil-related research. The first stirrings of political debate had surfaced somewhat earlier. At the meeting of the party's National Assembly in October 1971, Isobel Lindsay (vice-chairman for publicity), proposed the so-called 'Three Steps to Freedom' strategy, in which a devolved assembly and then control of the oil would be preliminary steps to the achievement of full independence.

It was clear that this gradualist strategy had not met with universal approval. At the March meeting of the National Council, a resolution from the Lenzie branch supporting the physical disruption of the flow of oil unless Scotland gained full control of it appeared on the agenda, suggesting a 'militant tendency' within the party on the oil issue. On the other hand, a report to the National Assembly from the research officer (Donald Bain), on the political significance of the issue, made the case for a moderate line. It argued that while oil proved Scotland's economic viability 'beyond all doubt', the U.K. government was not likely to relinquish control of such a valuable asset lightly, and a get-tough policy towards the oil companies would only be counter-productive. It was in the party's interests to tread carefully.[12]

These differences came to a head at the party's annual conference in May 1972. The first three resolutions on the conference agenda concerned the issue. Most attention was focused on the proposal from Gordon Wilson, which restated the Lindsay/Bain arguments by linking control of North Sea oil to the setting up of a Scottish Assembly (tentatively promised by the Conservative government). It was the coupling of oil demands with a pro-devolutionary position on self-government which was to prove controversial. It was bound to precipitate opposition from traditionalists who objected to devolution under any circumstances. Thus, the debate centred around the devolutionary implications of the resolution rather than whether the party had a legitimate interest in the oil issue or not. It was this which accounted for the relatively close vote on the decision to go ahead with the oil campaign.[13]

From then on, the timing and organisation of the campaign was controlled by the party's executive. Following a meeting of the N.E.C. on 30 June, the launch was scheduled for September. Preparations were made throughout the summer, including the production for the press of oil 'action packs' initially tested on delegates to the annual conference Douglas Crawford was given special responsibility within the campaign group for press releases and publicity, with Gordon Wilson occupying the positions of campaign director and the party's official spokesman on oil.

In identifying oil as a 'major new issue' for the nationalist case, Mr Wilson claimed that the opposition parties were 'already sensitive on the question of North sea oil, since they know it strikes a ready chord of resentment'.[14] He was not alone in this assessment. Jim Sillars, then Labour M.P. for South Ayrshire, argued in July that both Labour and Conservative parties were reluctant to give Scotland any special benefit from oil because of their 'haunting fear of nationalism', although the Labour Party in Scotland had actually approved two pro-Scottish measures on oil at its conference in March 1972. Mr Sillars's estimation may have been more appropriate in the case of the Conservative party, and Miller *et al.* claim that Conservative oil policy did not give any special favour to Scotland until 1973.[15] However, assessments about what might or might not be a 'pro-Scottish' oil policy very much depended on who was doing the judging. If there were other calls for a 'pro-Scottish' oil policy at this time, they were either not heard or were conflated with the S.N.P.'s own emerging position. Party strategists had at last found a winner. The party's special financial appeal circulated to all branch and constituency delegates attending the September National Council was thus fairly accurate when it said that oil gave the party 'one of its best ever opportunities of securing self-government'.[16]

The campaign group within the party had achieved a number of important objectives in the pre-launch phase. It had mobilised sufficient organisational resources to plan and run the campaign. It had secured a large measure of internal agreement that such a campaign was a good idea. It had successfully run a few pilot schemes, and had perceived that its opponents were vulnerable on the issue. But the supporters of an oil strategy had also moved cautiously, monitoring public and party reaction (in so far as this was possible) as they went. As the debate up to and including the 1972 party conference had shown, there was a division of opinion when it came to linking the oil issue to constitutional demands. While the endorsement of conference was important, it was not decisive in either ending opposition or in circumscribing the actions of the campaigners, as we shall see.

The first phase of the oil campaign

The 'It's Scotland's Oil' campaign was launched on 5 September 1972 with the official objectives of publicising the value of the oil reserves and informing Scots of the economic opportunities they created. But the campaign was not simply an ingenuous exercise to inform. As a piece of sophisticated political advertising, it had internally driven goals which had little to do with public information.

First, it was to serve as a means of building party membership. As has been the case with all S.N.P. issue campaigns, a recruitment drive was an integral part of the oil campaign. This was to be achieved through the distribution of oil 'action packs' and business reply cards to selected households (the latter innovation was one of the enduring legacies of the oil campaign). Second, it provided the party with a foundation on which to build up an economic case for independence, and, through the consistent use of a realistic set of figures gave the party an image of credibility and competence. Third, it sought to build a coalition of opinion around the party's position and so isolate the opposition. Finally, the campaign was seen as a general confidence-building enterprise for party activists in the localities, and voters in general.

The first press conference gave details of the S.N.P.'s estimates. On the basis of a peak annual production of 150 million tons worth an estimated £2,200 millions, it was calculated that the government would accrue £825 millions per annum in taxation revenues (a rate of 37·5% was assumed). If these revenues were included in the general figures for central government income and expenditure in Scotland, then income would far exceed expenditure, thus ending any fiscal reason for maintaining the Union from Scotland's point of view. Thus, the economic basis of the campaign was clear.

The press conference was followed immediately by a series of meetings all over Scotland, in which these figures were reiterated together with a warning that governments would spend the revenues on projects that were no use to Scotland unless action was taken to assert Scotland's 'right' to the oil. A week after the campaign had started, Gordon Wilson claimed that there had been a 'staggering response'. In line with the third 'internal' objective, 'Scottish-minded' organisations such as the Scottish Trades Union Congress, the Scottish Chambers of Commerce and the local authorities were invited to join in.[17] At the same time, the party began to probe the government's suspected weaknesses on the issue.

The first tactic was to send letters to the Prime Minister and the Secretary of State for Scotland challenging them to deny the S.N.P.'s figures and estimates. In one sense, there was nothing to argue about as the S.N.P. was using the same figures for annual production (150 million tons) that the minister responsible (George Younger), had already announced. But there was an apparent divergence of view in government circles. In June, Sir William McEwan Younger of British Petroleum and a former chairman of the Scottish Conservative Party, had quoted an annual production figure of 300–400 million tons achievable by the early 1980s. This was two to three times the official estimates. The government chose, wisely, to avoid getting into a dispute about production figures, and responded instead by disputing only the S.N.P.'s estimates concerning revenues. It claimed that revenues of £80 millions rather than £800 millions were more likely in 1980.

However, in trying to minimise the fiscal impact of the oil, the government laid itself open to the charge that it was selling the resource too cheaply. Indeed, this argument was subsequently taken up by both the S.N.P. and the Labour Party. The alternative was to admit that the S.N.P. was generally correct in identifying oil revenues as a major contributor to the U.K. exchequer, even if disputing the figures in detail. For the government was not necessarily the major loser in the S.N.P.'s campaign. If the S.N.P. could establish itself as the focus of opposition in Scotland, then it was the Labour Party which might suffer the most. The coalition-building element of the strategy was a clear attempt by the Nationalists to construct a 'Scottish' pole of opposition to the government in which they would be the major players.

If proof were needed, it became readily available when a by-election was called in the hitherto safe Labour seat of Dundee East some two months into the campaign. Occasioned by the elevation of the sitting M.P. to the House of Lords, the by-election provided an ideal opportunity for the Nationalists to gauge the salience of their campaign. It was immediately announced from S.N.P. headquarters that Gordon Wilson had been selected as the party's candidate, and the campaign, which had shown signs of flagging, started to pick up again. Press releases increased from about two per week prior to the announcement, to four to five per week in the weeks following.

There was hardly a better constituency in Scotland in which to test the effectiveness of the oil campaign on Labour voters. Dundee was adjacent to the exploration zones, yet had not really benefited a great deal from the oil boom. Thus, the economic nationalism of the S.N.P.'s campaign could be expected to find a sympathetic audience in Dundee. At the local political level, the party was blessed with the classic conditions in which third parties can expect to do well.[18] City politics were dominated by a decaying Labour machine and party competition was weak. The Conservative vote was traditionally low, while the S.N.P. had performed modestly at the 1970 general election. If the S.N.P. was making inroads into Labour support, then it would show up in Dundee East.

The party's use of the oil issue in the by-election campaign showed two perceptible changes from the policy agreed by conference. Gordon Wilson's adoption speech as prospective parliamentary candidate stated that the by-election would be fought on the inter-related themes of oil and self-government, and did not mention the 'assembly first' strategy debated and approved by conference. Scottish oil, said Mr Wilson, would only become

Scotland's oil with self-government. Second, there was a far greater readiness to attack the oil companies directly for 'profiteering' at Scotland's expense. At a stroke, Labour was robbed of any exclusivity when it came to attacking big business.

These new themes did not replace the original campaign themes, but were added to them. The S.N.P. took every opportunity to publicise its own figures, assert Scotland's 'right' to the oil and argue for a policy of restricted exploitation. Thus, it was claimed that the 1958 Geneva Convention and the 1968 Continental Shelf (Jurisdiction) order gave Scotland legal title. In arguing that it was not in Scotland's interest to see rapid exploitation of the reserves, the party was asserting that Scotland's national interests were in direct variance with the policies being pursued by the government. For this purpose, both major parties rather than the government exclusively came into the firing line. They were accused of colluding to hide the true extent of the reserves and of playing down their value. It was claimed that the 'London based' parties did not want to talk about North Sea oil, while Scottish opinion outside of the 'London based parties' was saying 'what the nationalist party has been maintaining for some time' concerning the potential benefits of North Sea oil for Scotland.[19] The impression was given that there was support for an S.N.P. style oil policy in every organisation in Scotland except the two major political parties.

The switch in emphasis onto attacking both major parties and the additions to the campaign were perfectly understandable in the context of the Dundee contest. As Labour held the seat, the Nationalists had to direct more of their fire onto the incumbent. This explains the attacks on the oil companies, as it was a theme which was likely to appeal to many Labour voters and was typically the kind of policy which Labour itself would advocate. By this means, the S.N.P. pre-empted any Labour claim that it was the only party which would 'get tough' with the oil companies. While this essentially went against the advice of the research officer, it can be seen as a reasonable response to the fortuitous turn of events. Similarly, by deliberately taking up a hard position on the constitutional issue, the Nationalists hoped to expose Labour's own hesitant and confused policy, or more accurately, its absence of a policy.

If it was hard to judge the effect on public opinion, there had certainly been a noticeable impact on the S.N.P.'s organisation. The Treasurer reported an increased workload at headquarters to the December National Council, and Gordon Wilson's report noted that 'thanks to the widespread support from members of the party and the public, the oil campaign has approached being an unqualified success'. A record number of leaflets had been sold to branches and constituency associations, in addition to 120,000 lapel stickers and thousands of posters. Sales of membership cards were running at double the level of the previous year, with many defunct branches starting to revive.[20]

Although the oil campaign was officially supposed to finish at the beginning of December, it was clear that it would be extended at least until the by-election was held. Extra publicity material was in preparation, and Gordon Wilson referred to the previous three months of campaigning as 'phase one'. The campaign moved into the new year with two further additions. First, there was less emphasis on the 'good news' aspect of the discoveries, and more on the reasons why Scotland could expect no substantial benefits from the oil under the present or any future U.K. government. The party claimed that Scotland was missing out on lucrative offshore supplies contracts, that it could only expect a share of the revenues commensurate with its share of the population in the U.K. total and that the government had been too lenient with the oil companies.

Second, in the absence of opinion poll data of any sort, the S.N.P. was to start creating its own. These amateur polls had three main advantages over their commercial counterparts: they were cheap, they involved party members and they gave the party an entirely free hand in setting the priorities it wanted. The 'oil survey' carried out in the Dundee East constituency linked the oil and constitutional questions together in a way which produced massive support for self-government. 1,200 voters were asked as a final question whether they thought the oil should be controlled by 'a democratically elected Scottish parliament', and it was perhaps of little surprise that 88% of the 'sample' favoured such an option.[21] The new policy had been instantly authenticated by public opinion.

The party also found a novel way to present its case, which purported to show that the oil would be worth thirty times its present value to a self-governing Scotland. Dundee was promised £28 millions for economic development alone as its 'share' of the revenues in an independent Scotland. The overall arguments were perhaps most cogently summarised by Gordon Wilson in the televised party political broadcast transmitted on 17 January. Against a backcloth of a map of the Scottish sector of the North Sea, Mr Wilson told viewers that Scotland was being 'bypassed by the big international oil companies in their haste to cream off the North Sea oil profits'. He said that the S.N.P. would be writing to the companies to outline 'realistic terms which would bring Scotland into line with other oil exporting countries' (Norway being the preferred model), on the subjects of taxation and royalties. Scotland could not afford to be soft or sentimental on these matters, he said, and must take the opportunity at the next election to demand the right to manage its own affairs.[22]

There was plenty of evidence that the other parties contesting Dundee were trying to ignore the oil issue. *The Times* reported that Gordon Wilson was 'the only candidate to whom North Sea oil is the dominant issue',[23] and although the S.N.P. did not win the by-election, it came very close to doing so. When the campaign was over, measurable organisational gains had been achieved in Dundee and elsewhere, and these were attributed to the oil campaign within the party. This impression was given added weight by Bochel and Denver's analysis of the Dundee result, which claimed to show that the party had doubled the size of its vote during the course of the campaign, taking two votes from Labour for every one it had taken from the Conservatives.[24] The accuracy or otherwise of these findings hardly mattered: the point was that the leading campaigners believed that the oil campaign had been responsible.

Thus, a great deal had been achieved by the end of the first phase. The general strategy worked out by oil group pragmatists and approved by conference had been vindicated. The party had increased its support, enlarged its membership and had taken a successful initiative on a new issue. The opposition parties had been shown to be vulnerable and without an effective counter strategy. The progress of the campaign also showed that conference decisions were only loosely adhered to by the campaign managers. The linkage between oil and devolution had been effectively abandoned, and a more aggressive stance had been taken towards the oil companies. Yet these two modifications sprang from completely different sources; while the former resulted essentially from internal opposition, the latter was designed to appeal to Labour voters in Dundee.

The development of the campaign

The final departure from the position agreed at the 1972 conference came in a new phase of the campaign announced a few days after the by-election. It was suggested that while oil could reverse Scotland's relative decline and alleviate social and economic privations, this would only happen if independence was achieved first. This effectively inverted the control-of-oil-first, independence-second strategy (with possible devolution in the middle), by saying that nothing short of independence would give

Scotland any control over the oil. Thus, not only had the idea of an intermediate oil-powered assembly been dropped (which had been the case for some time in fact), but independence was now formally elevated to the primary place. The research department was now concerned with devising a general post-independence economic policy rather than the oil strategy, although Gordon Wilson maintained that there was 'still a lot of running to be made on the oil issue'.[25]

The campaign generally and the Dundee contest in particular had caused a great rise in expectations within the party, resulting in a belief that independence was imminent. As there was little evidence either to confirm or deny these expectations, they became a reality which affected the content of decision making. In fact, no Scotland-wide survey of voting intentions had been held since 1970, although there were small Scottish sub-groups in the all-Britain surveys. It was on the basis of such evidence that Gordon Wilson claimed a 'trebling in support for the S.N.P. since the (oil) campaign was launched and the Dundee East by-election' at the National Council meeting in April 1973.[26] As the party could not afford to sponsor professional surveys, it had to rely either on national surveys sponsored by other organisations or on its own local and amateurish surveys and assessments.

However, even if relevant high quality public opinion data had been available, it is not certain to what use it would have been put. While some of those in and around the leadership would undoubtedly have argued that policy should be modified to fit public attitudes more closely, the majority were relatively uninfluenced by poll findings. Such, at least, was the perception of the leaders themselves, who regarded poll findings as little more than 'political footballs' which were generally ignored if they failed to confirm pre-existing prejudices, or upheld if they did.

The logic prevailing inside the party's organisation was a far more consistent influence on policy than poll findings were. Thus, the balmy climate induced by the apparent success of the first phase ensured a smooth and almost unnoticed passage for a new leadership initiative in 1973. In contrast to 1972, there was little evidence of either dissent or any new campaign at the 1973 annual conference. Speeches were made by the party chairman and by Gordon Wilson, and a resolution from Bearsden Branch and Central Dunbartonshire Association on the issue was passed unanimously. Opposition to the leadership's handling of the issue failed to materialise despite the numerous deviations which had been made from the policy agreed just one year previously.

The first official sign of a new campaign was in a circular from

Gordon Wilson to delegates attending the September meeting of the National Council. It said that the next phase must link up with the publication of the Kilbrandon Commission on the constitution, and would concentrate on the twin themes of Westminster mismanagement of the resource and the need for conservation. Just before the Council met, a press release announced that a new campaign would be launched 'in the autumn', which for all intents and purposes pre-empted any serious opposition at the National Council. In any case, there was no reason to expect any this time. A complex motion on campaign financing had also been prepared by the N.E.C. for approval by the delegates, who were told that the next stage must aim to project a strong and responsible image for the party. The timidity of the three month campaign proposed in 1972 had given way to one which was to last at least twice as long. The degree of advance planning in the campaign group and the certainty that this would be approved by the party membership (via the National Council) stood in marked contrast to the rather tentative nature of the development of the first campaign.

This does not mean that the party was more centralised in 1973 than it was in 1972. The basic structural relationships had not changed, and the generality of party members were no less influential than they had been. They did not really make a significant impact on policy in either year, or indeed any year in comparison with those who were members of the N.E.C., the National Council and the National Assembly, and those who dominated the proceedings of the annual conference. The only difference was that those who had raised criticism from within the elite of the nationally active in 1972 were quiescent in 1973.

The official campaign was launched on 5 September. It was designated as a pre-election campaign concentrating on the themes of land ownership, membership of the European Community, broadcasting and oil, with the last as the main plank as the campaign slogans reflected. In the latter half of October however, the campaign was overtaken by the imposition of unilateral increases in the price of crude oil, cuts in production and selected embargoes by the Arab members of O.P.E.C. For the first time, the party's oil policy carried perceptible costs as well as benefits. The trade-off was simple. Any softening of the party's position could be taken as a sign of weakness by opponents of the leadership both inside and outside the party. On the other hand, any closer identification of party policy with O.P.E.C. was likely to antagonise public opinion. The gains already made might then be lost.

The party was not without a choice of possible responses. It could press on with phase two of the campaign regardless of the

O.P.E.C. action – in other words, do nothing; it could intensify Scotland's claim to the oil in line with O.P.E.C.'s tough new position, or soften this stance in order to appear statesmanlike in time of crisis; it could drop the issue completely and campaign on something else.

The last option was probably the least viable alternative. The party could hardly stop talking about oil when it had become the preoccupation of politicians in every western state. In fact, its chosen course amounted to doing nothing. The campaign continued apparently unaltered, although the campaign slogan which had been planned before the O.P.E.C. action – 'Rich Scots or Poor British?' – took on a new and provocative significance. The vice-chairman for publicity reported that planned policy initiatives on both oil and devolution had been shelved not as a result of the O.P.E.C. action, but because of parliamentary by-elections in Glasgow Govan and Edinburgh North. Effort was conveniently diverted into what the party knew how to do best.[27]

Of the two constituencies, Govan proved to be a more favourable proposition despite the fact that the Party chairman was the candidate in Edinburgh North. There were some purely organis-ational reasons for this. The candidate in Govan (Margo MacDon-ald) had an excellent campaign machine at her disposal in comparison with Mr Wolfe in Edinburgh North. While the party's canvass returns predicted the narrow victory that was achieved in Govan, for example, they were wildly inaccurate in Edinburgh North.[28] But other factors were perhaps more important.

First, the party competitive and organisational politics of the Govan constituency were similar to those in Dundee East – but more so. The Labour Party totally dominated local politics in Govan. This dominance rested on the foundations of a decayed local party with an almost dynastic process of succession. Somewhat fortuitously for the S.N.P., the weaknesses of this system were fully exposed as it had produced a candidate who was unacceptable nationally. The chosen Labour candidate (Harry Selby), received little support from the party machine because of his known Trotskyist views. Just as in the 1988 Govan by-election, the byzantine nature of internal Labour politics worked to the S.N.P.'s advantage leaving disaffected Labour voters as easy prey.

The latter's status as easy prey, however, has to be seen in con-text. The Nationalists were able to take advantage of the situation because Labour voters were closer to the S.N.P. on the issues than they were to other parties. Irrespective of the differences in campaigning strength, Labour voters were far more likely to switch to the S.N.P. on policy grounds than the few Conservative voters were, as Miller's data on the Februrary 1974 election and Bochel and Denver's circumstantial evidence on the Dundee result showed. The salience of this point was illustrated by the result in Edinburgh North. As a solid Conservative seat with a moderate degree of party competitition in which the S.N.P. had not run a candidate in the 1970 election, it did not prove fertile nationalist soil on this occasion. Conservative voters would not switch to the S.N.P. as a form of protest when a Liberal candidate could and did fulfil this role in the constituency.[29]

The results strengthened the view that the party did not need to soften its position on oil. On the contrary, it seemed that a hard line was popular, especially with Labour voters. Thus, three weeks after the Govan victory, the party announced a 'change in direction in its successful oil campaign' in which the S.N.P. would be scrutinising the oil companies far more closely.[30] It is interesting, however, that this warning was set in the context of the Govan by-election rather than the upheavals in the middle east and world oil markets. This can best be explained as an attempt to retain a firm position on oil while at the same time avoiding identification with O.P.E.C. hate-figures such as Colonel Ghaddafi. The party had a new dilemma – how to deal with the argument that the oil campaign had appealed to the greed of the voters.

There was no consensus on this issue within the leadership, with the new tougher policy being supported by those who originally doubted the wisdom of an oil campaign. There were two reasons for their apparent change of heart. As the party had fudged the incremental strategy very early on in the first phase, oil and devolution were no longer linked in the campaign. Thus, its most obnoxious element had been removed to the satisfaction of constitutional hardliners. Secondly, as the current misgivings emanated from some of those who had supported the oil campaign in the first place, their opponents automatically took up the opposite view. Despite initial inaction and some differences in opinion within the party leadership, the oil crisis did result in the party taking a harder line towards both the government and the oil companies, at least in the short term.

This autarchic neo-O.P.E.C. position appeared in a detailed analysis of what rising oil prices would mean for a sovereign Scotland. According to the S.N.P., this confirmed the economic case for independence and made the choice of 'Rich Scots or Poor Britons? more inescapable than ever'.[31] It was even argued that this would be of benefit to England. As one of the few countries in Western Europe with secure oil supplies, an independent Scotland would sell oil to its neighbour at no more than it would pay for middle east supplies. Yet, while the post-Govan twist in the slow spiral of militancy on the oil issue may have been broadly appropriate in the context of the success achieved there, the party's ability to withdraw from these positions if public opinion demanded it had not yet been tested.

Eclipse and decline of the oil strategy

In fact, the winding down of the oil campaign was a direct result of the February 1974 general election. In the first place, the S.N.P. campaign itself provoked controversy within the party's leadership. Instead of carrying through the logic of the Govan campaign and appealing to Labour voters specifically, the party's election manifesto promised that the oil revenues could finance higher living standards, greately improved pensions, a reduced level of income tax, a five year 'holiday' from property taxes and a 4% interest rate on home loans provided that Scotland was self-governing.[32] As in the Dundee campaign, both major parties were criticised for creating a spurious debate over the ownership of North Sea oil while agreeing that it was a U.K. asset. Such a programme was hardly aimed at the more disadvantaged groups in society, and thus it was of no surprise that the S.N.P. concentrated campaigning resources in predominantly rural, Conservative-held seats. Second, with the installation of a minority Labour government and the election of seven S.N.P. M.P.s, oil became a secondary, almost minor question because the Nationalist M.P.s were thrust immediately into a pivotal role at Westminister. While the oil campaign did enter a new phase in June 1974 in anticipation of a fresh election, the whole issue went into a slow eclipse as the party, the electorate and Westminister became enmeshed in the devolution 'debate'. The whole change in circumstances had the inevitable effect of switching attention from the party in Scotland to the M.P.s at Westminister and splintering the leadership, an experience from which it did not profit as we will show.

Immediately after the February election, the 'Three Steps to Freedom' strategy made a faltering comeback, although the first stage (an elected assembly with limited powers), was now missing. The party was now showing official good will towards the Kilbrandon Commission findings, and Donald Stewart, the leader of the S.N.P. parliamentary group, pledged that he would take 'a helpful and responsible attitude at Westminister' in matters both Scottish and British.[33] The thinking behind this strategy seems to have been the belief that the electorate would react positively to hard-working, model M.P.s. The party's electoral performance became inextricably linked to the performance of its M.P.s.

Mr Wolfe stated in April that '(o)ur seven M.P.s not only hold the key to retaining their own seats; collectively, they carry much of the responsibility for maintaining and increasing the support which the party has throughout the country'. The 'Survey of Parliamentary Candidates' carried out by the research department reflected that these sentiments were general throughout the party.[34] The parliamentary group therefore copied the other parties by assigning various portfolios to individual group members, so creating a battery of spokespersons in a kind of shadow government format. Thus, the oil and devolution spokesmen (Gordon Wilson and George Reid respectively) became just components in an all round team which tried to address itself to all the issues of the day. As the parliamentary group got drawn into the web of bargaining resulting from the creation of a minority government, the oil issue naturally started to loss its centrality and undergo further modification.

Pressure came from a new source to modify the party's O.P.E.C-style policy. Apparently at the request of M.P.s from other parties, some S.N.P. members asked for the 'Rich Scots or Poor British?' poster to be withdrawn, and there was an attempt at the September meeting of the National Council to have the campaign dropped completely. This had followed a discussion of a remitted resolution from annual conference which had called for preferential treatment in the supply and pricing of oil for 'our neighbours in the British Isles' by a future S.N.P. government.[35] Some party members had evidently concluded that the direct appeal to self-interest inherent in the oil campaign had started to backfire, and that it was time to drop it.

Paradoxically, the Opinion Research Centre (O.R.C.) poll of Scottish voters carried out in April 1974, appeared to show that there was substantial support for the basic S.N.P. position on oil represented by the 'It's Scotland's oil' campaign: 66% of the sample agreed and 25% disagreed with the proposition that Scotland would get very little benefit from the oil compared to the oil companies and the U.K. government, 59% agreed with the proposition that North Sea oil belonged to Scotland and that the tax revenues from it 'should be used to benefit the Scottish people', and an overwhelming majority disagreed with the proposition that Scotland got 'more than a fair share of economic help from the British government'.[36] When these figures were broken down by party allegiance, a plurality of voters of all parties except the Conservatives, agreed with what was essentially a thinly disguised version of the S.N.P.'s original policy.

On the other hand, the poll did not indicate that there was support for O.P.E.C.-style militancy, as 60% also agreed with the proposition that the oil should be used to 'benefit all of Britain and not just Scotland alone'. Thus the poll could not be seen as an unqualified vindication of the recent positions the party had taken. As it also confirmed that Labour voters were closer to the S.N.P. on the issues than voters of other parties, it strengthened the case for attacking the Labour vote by softening the oil policy perhaps to its original form, and giving a more social democratic flavour to the party's propaganda.

Such a move involved quite a substantial change in priorities and was at the nub of the disagreements within the leadership. The neo-O.P.E.C. policy so recently adopted would have to be modified, and so would the party's deployment of campaign resources. Judging by the presentation of the oil issue in October, it seems that such a change was effected to some degree. The October election manifesto was sub-titled 'A Programme for Social Democracy', and said that the S.N.P. would use the oil revenues to solve urgent social problems such as poor housing, to help disadvantaged groups and to provide increased aid for the third world, with which Scotland was identified, at least in spirit.[37] This stood in stark contrast to the February programme, which by promising to reduce taxation, addressed itself to wealthier groups in society.

The S.N.P. moved only so far towards Labour, however. It continued to criticise both parties for being insufficiently Scottish rather than singling out the Labour party for being insufficiently socialist. The O.R.C. survey had shown that the party's main appeal was on specifically Scottish rather than class issues, and that it had drawn support from across the social spectrum. If it had been trying to project a strongly nationalist image, then it had been successful at doing so. The question of the party's future ideological direction was discussed at the December meeting of the National Council, and revealed there was a continuing lack of consensus. As may have been expected, those in favour of a more leftist orientation were part of the leadership in Scotland, with the M.P.s, predominantly sitting in former Conservative-held seats, generally tending to take a centrist position on social questions.[38]

As the S.N.P. got bogged down in the devolution versus independence debate which came to occupy so much time between 1975 and 1979, the oil campaign was relegated in importance. Support for the oil policy gradually declined between 1974 and 1979 as Miller *et al.* (1980) have shown. Thus, it may be that those who had already sensed that the campaign had started to backfire were correct. On the other hand, it can be argued that support fell away because of the change in the status of the campaign, which effectively conceded defeat to the party's opponents. There was no evidence that the policy was unpopular in 1974: on the contrary, there was every indication that it was popular. Thus, there was no need to change it by this criterion, yet it was changed on many occasions.

It is ironic that the party had managed to run an apparently successful campaign for two years without the aid of survey data, but that as soon as this did start to appear regularly in the media, the party continually lost ground on the issue. However skilled the S.N.P. campaigners may have appeared to be, they gained little benefit from an accurate flow of information on the state of public opinion, on this issue at least. But this was not the root of the problem. The doubts which surfaced over the policy in 1974 had little to do with the party's objective standing in the opinion polls, and were rather a product of internal debate in the leadership, successful pressure from competitor parties, and the structural changes in the party leadership resulting from the creation of the parliamentary group.

In summary, the party clearly had a problem in adapting its strategy successfully after the initial phase. The very existence of the oil campaign showed that the party was capable of 'rational' behaviour. However, it also showed that even on seemingly low cost, high benefit issues, internal and external constraints exercised an enormous influence on party strategy. Conversely, the impact of objective survey data on policy decisions seemed to be inconsistent and sporadic in this case. Ideas about what was popular inside the party and the electorate originated from subjective assessments and other non-scientific analyses, and were generated primarily within the confines of the party's policy making elite. Finally, it seems that the oil campaign was seen as a device for expanding the party's organisational format rather than transforming it. While the desired electoral growth was achieved, the organisational implications of it were not fully appreciated. Thus, the party remained firmly wedded to the 'mass party' model, and to the consequences it entailed.

Notes

1 Lee (1976) argues that the S.N.P.'s 'It's Scotland's Oil' campaign 'was probably the most successful ever launched there', G. Lee, 'North Sea oil and Scottish nationalism', *Political Quarterly*, 47, 3, pp. 307–317, 1976. For support of the 'positive' view, see also K. Webb, *The Growth of Nationalism in Scotland*, Harmondsworth, Penguin, 1978, pp. 157–62. Bogdanor (1981) takes the opposite view arguing that the survey evidence proved that 'It's Scotland's Oil was not a success' as it only appealed to those who supported the party anyway; V. Bodganor, *Devolution*, Oxford, Oxford University Press, 1979, p. 98.

2 On the party's electoral performance and figures for membership during this period, see Tables 17a, 17b and 19b respectively in J. G. Kellas, *The Scottish Political System* (3rd edn) Cambridge, Cambridge University Press, 1984, pp. 135 and 142.

3 W. L. Miller, *The End of British Politics?, Scots and English Political Behaviour in the 1970s*, Oxford, Oxford University Press, 1981, p. 121.

4 Miller, *The End of British Politics?*, p. 60.

5 See report in the *Glasgow Herald*, 22 October 1970.

6 Resolution to the National Council from Edinburgh North and Forres branches, ref. NC/71/38, Scottish National Party, Edinburgh, 12 June 1971.

7 See report in *The Scotsman*, 13 September 1971.

8 Miller argues that 'the S.N.P. was reluctant to take up the issue and only joined in a campaign which others had started' because it was seen by many as merely 'pressure group' politics, Miller, *The End of British Politics?*, p. 59.

9 Interestingly, this resolution was proposed by the party branch which had been most involved in the by-election campaign. Resolution to the National Council from Stirling St Ninian's branch, ref. NC/71/57, Scottish National Party, Edinburgh, 25 September 1971.

10 Chairman's report to the National Council, Scottish National Party, Edinburgh, 4 December 1971.

11 See report in *The Scotsman*, 30 December 1971.

12 Minutes of the National Assembly, ref. NA/72/15 and NA/72/16, Scottish National Party, Edinburgh, 9 April 1972.

13 The vote in favour of the resolution was 93–76. See reports in *The Scotsman*, 27 and 29 May 1972, *The Guardian*, 27 May 1972.

14 Report to the National Council, Scottish National Party, Edinburgh, 20 July 1972.

15 See report in *The Scotsman*, 10 July 1972; W. Miller, J. Brand and M. Jordan, *Oil and the Scottish Voter 1974–79*, London, Social Science Research Council, 1980, ch. 1.

16 Circular for oil appeal fund, Scottish National Party, Edinburgh, 2 September 1972.

17 See report in the *Glasgow Herald*, 12 September, 1972.

18 See M. Pinard, *The Rise of the Third Party: A Study in Crisis Politics*, New Jersey, Prentice Hall, 1971, part 2 esp.

19 See Press release no. 517, Scottish National Party, Edinburgh, 14 November 1972, and Press release no. 529, Scottish National Party, Edinburgh, 30 November 1972. See report in *The Times*, 22 November 1972; Press release no. 520, Scottish National Party, Edinburgh, 20 November 1972, Press release no. 522, Scottish National Party, Edinburgh, 22 November 1972.

20 Treasurer's report to the National Council, Scottish National Party, Edinburgh, 2 December 1972. See report by Gordon Wilson to the National Council, Scottish National Party, Edinburgh, 2 December 1972, and report by the

executive vice-chairman for organisation to the National Council, minute of the National Council ref. NC/72/52, Scottish National Party, Edinburgh, 2 December 1972.

[21] See Press release no. 568, Scottish National Party, Edinburgh, 9 February 1973.

[22] See Press release no. 551, Scottish National Party, Edinburgh, 10 January 1973.

[23] See report in *The Times*, 21 February, 1973.

[24] See report in *The Scotsman*, 13 March 1973. It was reported to the National Council in December that 100 new members had been recruited in Dundee East already, and the Treasurer's report to the March meeting noted an upturn in income to H.Q. resulting from membership growth; National Council minute ref. NC/72/53, Scottish National Party, Edinburgh, 2 December 1972 and Treasurer's report to the National Council, Scottish National Party, Edinburgh, 14 April 1973. The report by Gordon Wilson to the National Council in April attributed the party's success to the oil campaign; Report by Gordon Wilson to the National Council, Scottish National Party, Edinburgh, 14 April 1973.

[25] Report by Gordon Wilson to the National Council, Scottish National Party, Edinburgh, 14 April 1973.

[26] Ibid.

[27] 'The press issues on which we had planned to concentrate during the autumn were oil and the Kilbrandon report, but the by-elections have, of course, dictated our press strategy. Decisions on our campaign in the New Year must await the election results.' Report by vice-chairman for publicity to the National Council, Scottish National Party, Edinburgh, 1 December, 1973. See also report in *The Scotsman*, 31 October 1973.

[28] It is noteworthy that Alex Ewing, a leading critic of the oil strategy at the 1972 annual conference, played an influential role in the Govan campaign. Mr Ewing was quoted as saying that the oil campaign was 'proving to be a massive S.N.P. success'; see report in the *Glasgow Herald*, 18 December 1973.

[29] Miller, *The End of British Politics?*, pp. 122–123 especially.

[30] See Press release, Scottish National Party, Edinburgh, 28 November 1973.

[31] See Press release, Scottish National Party, Edinburgh, 17 December 1973.

[32] See Press release no. 754, Scottish National Party, Edinburgh, 6 February 1974. See reports in the *Glasgow Herald*, 8 and 15 February 1974.

[33] See Press release, Scottish National Party, Edinburgh, 7 March 1974 and Press release, Scottish National Party, Edinburgh, 4 April 1974.

[34] Chairman's report to the National Council, Scottish National Party, Edinburgh, 20 April 1974.

[35] Chairman's report to the National Council, Scottish National Party, Edinburgh, 15 June 1974.

[36] Proceedings of the 40th Annual conference, 31 May 1974. See reports in the *Glasgow Herald*, 30 May 1974 and *The Guardian*, 3 June 1974.

[37] See report in *The Scotsman*, 14 May, 1974.

[38] 'Scotland's Future', West Calder, S.N.P. Publications, September 1974. For the arguments in favour of a more leftist orientation, see Chairman's report to the National Council, Scottish National Party, Edinburgh, 7 December 1974 and also Senior vice-chairman's report to the National Council, Scottish National Party, Edinburgh, 7 December 1974; the case against was put by Douglas Crawford; see Executive vice-chairman's report to the National Council, Scottish National Party, Edinburgh, 7 December 1974. On the M.P.s' orientation generally see W. Mishler and A. Mughan, 'Representing the Celtic Fringe: Devolution and Legislative Behaviour in Scotland and Wales; *Legislative Studies Quarterly*, 3, 3, 1978, pp. 377–408 and also A. Fusaro, 'Two Faces of British Nationalism: The S.N.P. and P.C. compared', *Polity*, 11, 3, 1979, pp. 362–386.

CHAPTER 4

Devolution and Destabilisation

The constitution of the S.N.P. states simply that the party's aim is 'Self government for Scotland', which is defined as the achievement of national sovereignty within the world community of nations.[1] The problem has always been to convince the majority of voters in Scotland of the desirability of this objective. The S.N.P. has never had majority approval for its central goal, as support for complete independence has hovered around about the 20% level since surveys have been conducted on the same issue.[2] Thus, the party has had the choice of either modifying its position in some way, seeking out other issues to build up support or resigning itself to permanent minority status.

It would be curious indeed if the party did not wish the constitutional issue to occupy the centre of political debate. Ideally, this would happen under circumstances where the majority of the Scottish electorate had been converted to the cause of independence. So far, this has never proved to be the case. Thus, on the few occasions when this issue has assumed political importance, the S.N.P. has been forced to address the central strategic problem inherent in its programme.

The oil campaign showed that the S.N.P. was not so dogmatic that it was either unwilling or unable to exploit other issues. The point was how far this pragmatism could be stretched. In circumstances where the party occupied an unpopular position – as on the question of independence – the rational strategy was to make a convincing shift of position towards the majority, even though this would entail organisational costs. Such an adjustment would best be made when it inflicted least damage on the party structure. As we have argued however, third parties like the S.N.P. are relatively more open and competitive than their rivals, and have severe difficulties making such adjustments.

58

There is a further complication. In his study of government formation, Luebbert (1984) argues that problems of adjustment may be exacerbated by the complexity of the issue in question. He suggests that party leaders are least threatened where issues are concerned only with broad principles of direction. On the other hand, issues that 'concern timing, amounts, rates of change . . . and further programmatic elaboration of previously established principles . . . almost always generate dissension'.[3]

While the oil policy gradually achieved this status, devolution was always problematic in this sense. The advent of the 'great devolution debate' in 1974 simply brought it to a head. The party entered a new phase in its development, one where it had to abjure 'movement' politics and embrace the politics of 'bargaining'. The ability to overcome internal constraints on rational behaviour at this stage is perhaps a greater mark of organisational maturity than the ability to mount popular, but rather vague campaigns. Yet the S.N.P.'s involvement with the devolution issue provides a graphic example of how constraining variables prevent the successful adaptation by third parties to market conditions. Devolution was difficult to deal with because it focused attention sharply on the party's doctrine of national sovereignty, which even those in favour of some compromise would not renounce. As many have argued the party was never unanimous in its support for a devolved assembly[4] and the introduction of legislative proposals simply made a latent division active. This became further aggravated with the passage of those proposals.

However, devolution should not have been seen as an entirely negative issue. First, the party stood to gain electoral benefits if it could manage to construct a popular policy. Secondly, devolution involved constitutional rule changes that were potentially beneficial for third parties. While it was a response designed by the major parties to win back votes from the Nationalists, as Kellas (1976) and others have argued,[5] the creation of an elected assembly in Scotland would have given the S.N.P. another platform from which to argue its case and potentially involved it in the exercise of some limited executive power.

The party did not seek to avoid the issue – indeed, it is difficult to see how it could have done so – and it did try to move to a more popular position. However, it was not successful in this venture. It failed to convince voters of its moderation, while at the same time paying the price of moderation through divisions within its own ranks. The constraints on rational behaviour stemming from the party's minority position, its organisational structure and its fundamental immaturity proved to be overwhelming.

Its attempts to adapt its strategy can be broken down into three distinct phases, within which it oscillated between voter opinion and the preferred opinion among the generality of decision makers. While neither was static, there was a cyclical movement in policy between these notional polarities, and after an initial movement towards mainstream public opinion, the party progressively drifted away from it as internal politics took over.

The first phase (1974–76), was characterised by the most serious attempt at adaptation, in which a fundamental change in policy could have been permanently effected at minimal organisational cost. After making the difficult decision however, there was a rapid drift back towards the preferred option of independence. The second phase (1976–77) represented a reclamation period which was largely unsuccessful, and the final phase (1977–78), saw a downward spiral into demoralisation and decay as the party experienced increasing amounts of internal dissension. We will first review the immediate background to the party's involvement with devolution, and then trace the party's attempt to devise a rational strategy in the context of its rate of growth, the state of internal conflict and the capacity of the leadership to make rational decisions.

Internal debate, 1971–74

The party's difficulties with the issue of devolved government or 'home rule' as it used to be called, are perennial and endemic. However, the revival, or more accurately, the take-off in S.N.P. fortunes in the late 1960s and early 1970s made the resolution of these problems a matter of some significance for British politics. In the period immediately prior to the publication of the Kilbrandon report and the election of a minority Labour government in 1974, the case for a gradualist strategy had been made in a paper submitted to the party's National Assembly in 1971. It argued that because the electorate was basically suspicious of change, it would always support the status quo if its only other choice was a completely separate state:

> the idea of the S.N.P. declaring U.D.I. on achieving a majority of M.P.s is not only terrifying to the electorate, but it is also very arrogant . . . we must not give the electorate the choice of voting for a united Britain or a separate Scotland . . . I feel as a matter of priority we state now that we accept the idea of achieving self government through the use of a temporary phase of internal self-government[6]

This approach abandoned the so-called 'mandate' strategy, which consisted of waiting until S.N.P. candidates were elected in a majority of Scotland's parliamentary constituencies and then declaring independence. It would remove the fear of change by supporting an idea ('home rule') that politicans in various parties had been advocating for years. The crux of the problem was that this would not be popular within the party, and the debates on the oil policy and on resolution 31 at the 1972 Annual Conference showed the level of conflict which an affirmation of devolution could create.

Resolution 31 stated that the party would 'wholeheartedly accept all devolutionary concessions wrung from Westminister as steps on the road to independence', affirmed the basic goal of independence and rejected Scottish membership of any Association of British States. Even though the devolutionary element was accepted (despite attempts to delete it), the whole resolution was remitted back to the National Council for further discussion where the issue remained for the rest of the year.[7] When the party's National Assembly decided early in 1973 to dissociate the party from the Conservative's plan for devolved government and concentrate on independence instead, it showed that if the party was confronted by any actual 'devolutionary concessions' it rejected them anyway.

It can be argued that the oil policy represented the party's position on devolution, embodying as it did the 'Three Steps to Freedom' model referred to earlier. Margo MacDonald's report to the meeting of the National Council in April 1973, claiming that the S.N.P. had been holding the initiative on devolution was probably a reference to this. As we have shown however, this aspect of the oil policy was a non-starter from the beginning. But there was not much need for the party to have a specific policy on devolution at this time for two reasons: the Kilbrandon Commission on the constitution had not yet reported and the party had no influence at Westminster anyway.

Plans were made for some kind of initiative on devolution to coincide with the publication of the Kilbrandon report on the constitution in late 1973. In a document entitled 'Pre-election campaign: Oil and self-Government' and circulated to the delegates attending the September meeting of the National Council, Gordon Wilson said that the party must take advantage of the debate generated by the appearance of the report in order to put the case for self-government.[8] This hardly indicated that the party had become a convert to devolution, but in any case, no initiative ever materialised. Part of the explanation was undoubtedly the oil crisis and the by-election campaigns at Govan and Edinburgh North, but these priorities also betrayed a diffidence towards the whole question which the party always seemed to show.

The Kilbrandon proposals for Scotland entailed the creation of an elected assembly which would broadly have control over those matters currently administered by the Scottish Office, within the framework of the overall sovereignty of Westminster. On the face of it, this looked like a 'devolutionary concession' which the S.N.P. could 'wholeheartedly support'. The first reaction by the National Council however, took the form of a resolution from the N.E.C. to the December meeting, urging the Scottish Trades Union Congress (S.T.U.C.) to join the S.N.P. in demanding an extension of the economic and financial powers of the assembly proposed by the report. The bracing tone of the resolution showed that there was still little inclination to modify the party's basic policy on sovereignty, and indeed there was no change until the following April. Thus, the party entered the election without any agreed policy on devolution, but in this it was no different from any of its rivals, and could not really be at any special disadvantage. In any case, devolution was not the critical issue at this time for either the S.N.P. or the other parties. As we have argued, for almost two years the S.N.P.'s major campaigning issue had been oil, and this neatly coincided with the wider issues which dominated the February campaign throughout the U.K. The S.N.P.'s emphasis was only beginning to change at the start of 1974.

The dilemma of success

After the election, however, the party started to take a serious interest in devolution for two interrelated reasons. First, the incoming Labour government promised to produce devolution proposals of its own (which it did in the summer of 1974), and secondly, it did not have an overall majority in the House of Commons, and thus was potentially dependent on the smaller parties to sustain it in office. Not only did the S.N.P. now have a parliamentary party of seven M.P.s, but this group was also in a position of power. While these changes altered the party's leadership structure fundamentally by shifting attention away from Scotland and towards Westminster as we have argued, they additionally rendered useless the party's basic policy on sovereignty. The S.N.P. would hardly improve its credibility among Scottish voters by absenting itself from the political marketplace on the first occasion when it could exert some influence. In this sense, it had little choice but to reconsider its position.

As with the creation of the parliamentary group itself, the failure to plan an iitermediate strategy in advance was evident in the party's ad hoc response to its success. Immediately after his election as parliamentary group leader, Donald Stewart put forward three demands, including the creation of a Scottish assembly 'with control over economic expansion, oil and fish' as the price of S.N.P. support, and by April, the 'assembly' had become a 'Scottish parliament' with all existing Scottish Office powers, full economic and fiscal powers, and control over U.K. government departments in so far as their activities affected Scotland. Scotland was to have independent international representation and was to retain all 71 M.P.s and its U.K. cabinet place.[9]

While the party prefaced its demands by a pledge to play a 'helpful and constructive role', its shopping list went far beyond both the Kilbrandon proposals for an elected assembly and anything the government was likely to implement. The statement did not preclude the party from either considering or accepting something less however, and the party chairman's call for moderation in his report to the April meeting of the National Council was reinforced by the findings of two opinion polls, published in February and April respectively, which showed that support for independence had changed little from 1970 at around 20% of the electorate.[10]

It might have been expected therefore, that the annual conference would attempt to examine all the options available and decide on a coherent policy. Insofar as devolution was discussed at all, the debate centred on fundamental principles rather than concrete strategies. An emergency resolution moved by the party president calling on the government to hold a referendum on a devolution plan closely resembling the S.N.P.'s April position had to be abandoned, even though its supporters claimed that the proposals amounted to independence anyway, and calls were made instead for the party to reaffirm its commitment to 'full independence'.[11]

Thus, it is evident that conference had been ill-prepared by the leadership to consider the full policy implications of electoral success. The absence of a coherent plan stood in marked contrast to the preparation which had preceded the oil campaign. The April policy had been essentially concocted by a few senior figures in the party, and it was hardly surprising that conference delegates were easily mobilised around the party's pre-existing position. Thus, the party was farther away from a devolution strategy in June than it had been in April.

The June meeting of the National Council did not improve matters either. The report from the chairman on the findings of the survey carried out by the Opinion Research Centre (O.R.C.) for *The Scotsman* in April was self-congratulatory rather than analytical, and it was stated that oil and self-government were 'quite clearly' S.N.P. issues.[12] Whatever this was supposed to mean, it could not include the proposition that the S.N.P. had the most popular policy on self government. The survey findings showed that S.N.P. voters were a highly deviant category on the self government issue (Table 1).[13]

Table 1
Voter preferences for constitutional change

Option	All (%)	Con (%)	Lab (%)	Lib (%)	SNP (%)
(1) Keep the present system	21	24	23	12	2
(2) A Scottish Council of local authority representatives responsible to Westminster	19	24	24	21	6
(3) An elected assembly to handle domestic affairs responsible to Westminster	24	29	23	29	14
(4) A Scottish Parliament responsible for all Scottish affairs including economic ones, independent of Westminster which would be responsible for defence, foreign and international economic affairs.	16	10	17	20	23
(5) Complete independence	17	3	9	6	55
Don't know	3	1	4	2	–

The approximate range of S.N.P. policy coincided with options (4) and (5), and when those supporting these options are combined, it showed that there was a massive disparity between S.N.P. and other voters: while 78% of S.N.P. voters supported these options, a maximum of only 26% of voters of any other party did. Barring any shift of opinion towards the S.N.P., the party would have to modify its policy in order to occupy the majority position. Yet, even this strategy could not guarantee an increase in support, because self-government was a only secondary issue for Labour and Conservative voters, and the primary issue for S.N.P. voters, as the Chairman pointed out.[14] Thus, a moderate strategy carried the risk of creating disaffection among S.N.P. supporters without any corresponding rise in support elsewhere.

When the government's consultative document on devolution was published in June, there was some evidence of a further softening of the party's position. Iain MacCormick, the S.N.P.

member of parliament for Argyll, stated that the S.N.P.'s position was now 'fairly close' to that of the Liberal Party, and said that the party accepted that 'any kind of devolution in Scotland will be achieved stage by stage'.[15] But this view was not reflected by other party spokesmen. In a press statement issued two days later, Donald Stewart referred only to the party's own version of devolution, and made no concession to any lesser schemes. This harder line was reflected in statements by Margo McDonald and William Wolfe later on in the summer, and the party sent a deputation to the Scottish Office to meet the Minister of State, Lord Hughes, to seek further powers for an assembly.

The Labour government's own proposals were set out in a White Paper published in September which esesntially reiterated Kilbrandon's recommendations.[16] This placed the government right in the middle of the spectrum of opinion on devolution (option 3 in *The Scotsman* surveys), which, if the survey findings were correct, was the position supported by more people than any other option. So long as opinion did not polarise towards the extremes, the government could expect to gain the support of some of the adjacent groups for its own proposals and split off all those in favour of devolution from those in favour of complete separation. Such indeed was the intention of the whole devolution policy according to Miller (1979), Drucker and Brown (1980) and Keating and Barry-Jones (1982).[17]

However, this did not happen in the short term. Support for the S.N.P. and for both kinds of elective devolution, but particularly stronger devolution, rose in the run-up to the October general election. Giving exactly the same choice as the April survey, *The Scotsman*'s September O.R.C. survey showed that overall support for options (4) and (5) had increased among voters of all parties (from 33% to 44%), 47% of Liberal voters and 32% of Labour voters now supported either strong devolution or independence, and the proportion of the electorate intending to vote S.N.P. had risen quite sharply too.[18]

Thus, the S.N.P. entered the election period on a wave of rising support for itself and for stronger devolution in general. In any case, it did not really matter whether the party had an agreed devolution policy or not, as Miller (1981) shows that most voters thought the S.N.P. was in favour of an assembly.[19] The constitutional issue was given precedence over all other campaigning themes including oil. In an eve of poll assessment, William Wolfe described the election as a 'decisive step to self-government for Scotland', and George Reid's list of priorities for S.N.P. M.P.s in the new parliament dealt exclusively with devolution. After the results, Donald Stewart announced that the enlarged parliamentary group would be seeking a 'gilt-edged commitment' from the government on a timetable to establish an assembly, despite the fact that the party had not agreed on such a policy.[20]

The Commitment to Devolution, 1974–75

While generalities may have sufficed in the interregnum between campaigning and legislation, this position was untenable in the longer term. The issue was brought to a head in the post-mortem on the October 1974 election, which revealed a split between those who advocated a further broadening of the S.N.P.'s appeal towards Labour voters, and those who argued against any bias towards the left or right of the political spectrum. The Chairman's report to the December meeting of the National Council pointed out that Labour had actually increased its vote in thirty constituencies between February and October, and stated that the S.N.P. 'must not antagonise' Labour Party and trade union leaders and should play a full part in the labour movement. Supporting this position, Margo MacDonald argued that the S.N.P. had yet to convince working people that the S.N.P. 'is on their side'.[21]

The logic of this argument was fairly straightforward. First, Labour was the majority party in Scotland, and second, Conservative voters were consistently more 'unionist' on the constitutional question than Labour voters were, so there was little point in appealing to them. Therefore, the S.N.P. must attack the Labour vote in order to achieve further growth. One of the consequences of such a strategy was the adoption of a devolution policy which was broadly in harmony with Labour's own position. It was this issue as much as the future ideological direction of the party which was at the root of the debate.

Following this meeting, there was increasing evidence that the 'pro-devolutionists' had got their way. A document entitled 'A Scottish Assembly', circulated to all delegates at a meeting of the party's National Assembly in January, called upon the Labour government to carry out its manifesto pledge to set up a devolved assembly, and expressed the S.N.P.'s willingness to co-operate as 'full self government has not yet gained a majority mandate from the Scottish electors'.[22] The party promised not to obstruct either the establishment or the operation of an assembly so long as it had sufficient power. But while party spokesmen insisted that the S.N.P. would only support 'genuine devolution', it was not clear what it would do if a 'lesser' assembly was set up.

The debate thus far within the leadership must be placed in the context of the confused state of opinion in the party as a whole.

The Executive Vice-Chairman for organisation (Brian Innes-Will), reported to the March meeting of the National Council that the officers of local party branches displayed 'a remarkable lack of knowledge both of policy and party structure',[23] an ignorance which must have been particularly intense on devolution as the party had no coherent policy anyway. The decision therefore, to set up an N.E.C. sub-committee to deal with the matter and feature a major item on the S.N.P.'s attitude towards the proposed Scottish Assembly at the Party's annual conference, can be seen as an attempt to create a coherent climate of opinion which would endorse the new thinking. Unlike 1974, the leadership was making careful preparations to achieve a desired change of direction.

This whole episode confirms the view that disputes over policy did not originate from within the ranks of the ordinary party membership, and came instead from within the policy-making elite. Membership 'opinion' was nevertheless a vital resource to be mobilised by those promoting contending positions. Thus, according to the National Secretary, the policy approved by conference would be followed by the parliamentary group when the government's own proposal came before the House. The result of the N.E.C.'s preparations was conference resolution 17, endorsed by the National Council, which stated that:

> A. This conference resolves that the S.N.P. will participate fully in any Scottish Assembly which is democratically elected and will conduct an all out campaign to gain a majority of assembly seats, and that its objectives in doing so will be to make a constructive contribution in those limited areas of responsibility likely to be given to the assembly by the present Westminister government, and to work vigorously to extend the assembly's powers until it becomes a real Scottish parliament capable of serving effectively in the interests of the Scottish people.[24]

It was passed by an overwhelming majority despite an attempt by the traditionalists to have it remitted back, and this undoubtedly represented a major shift in policy for two reasons. First, the only condition now for S.N.P. participation in a Scottish assembly was that it should be democratically elected. Thus, the ambiguity over the S.N.P.'s attitude to a 'lesser' assembly was ended. Although part B of the resolution set out a full battery of economic powers which the party thought the assembly should have, these were no longer the decisive conditions. Secondly, the party was now committed to turn the assembly into 'a real Scottish Parliament' by stages. When interviewed at the start of the conference, William Wolfe said that the electorate would find it 'easier to understand the progress from the present situation via an assembly to a sovereign parliament, than a sweeping change from the status quo to an independent parliament'.[25]

This moved the party's position much closer to the centre of the devolution spectrum, while maintaining its appeal for those who favoured the stronger options. The party was now firmly committed to the evolutionary road to independence in which a devolved assembly would play a key role. While it should be remembered that almost two hundred delegates voted for the remit, the conference decision represented a major coup for the pro-devolutionists achieved at a minimal organisational cost.[26] Thus, the strategy before the hallmarks of a rational response to a minority policy by those who held power in the leadership. Not only was the policy altered to suit the majority of preferences within the electorate, but the change was effected in an organisationally efficient way.

The strategy in practice

The problem was that this did not signify a permanent and irreversible shift in party policy for two reasons. First, S.N.P. voters and supporters remained an extremely deviant category on the devolution question. Although a new O.R.C. survey showed that there had been a marginal increase in support for 'strong' devolution/independence since October (from 44% to 45%), and that there was now a clear majority among voters of all parties for an elected assembly (the S.N.P.'s new minimum condition), a majority of S.N.P. voters favoured independence while an overwhelming majority of all other voters did not. 55% of the S.N.P. sample favoured this option compared with 9% of Liberal and Labour supporters, and 4% of Conservative supporters.[27] Was it realistic therefore, for the S.N.P. to pose as the party of devolution when most of its supporters actually favoured independence?

Secondly, party spokesmen both inside and outside parliament did not seek to promote the party's minimum conditions as its central theme. In July for example, George Reid argued that it was in 'everyone's interest that the government adopt a maximalist approach right from the start' and Margo MacDonald contrasted real nationalists with devolutionist 'tinkerers'. In a debate in the House, Margaret Bain did seek to follow the conference policy, but Douglas Henderson swiftly reeled off a list of powers which he considered necessary unless the assembly was to be 'a laughing stock'. The party chairman, William Wolfe said that the S.N.P.

stood for an assembly 'with wide ranging powers' compared to the government's 'provincial assembly', although he did say that the government's plan provided a 'basic framework for the advance of independence'.[28] However, the balance of propaganda clearly served to highlight the preference for 'strong' devolution and independence.

The party's new campaign launched in September focused on the economic case for independence by 'contrasting what is under a Westminster government and what could be under a Scottish parliament', and at a meeting in Edinburgh, Gordon Wilson argued that an assembly with real powers 'means independence . . . there can be no half way house'. The Chairman's report to the National Council stated that Kilbrandon style assembly 'would not be acceptable' and that Scotland was 'entitled to a National Assembly' which only the S.N.P. could achieve. In noting the near S.N.P. majority among voters under 35, Mr Wolfe argued that this 'would give us an uncontestable mandate to establish a sovereign Scottish parliament and an independent constitution'.[29]

These statements were completely at variance with the decisions made at conference, and did nothing to reinforce the image of moderation constructed there. An unadorned elected assembly was supposed to be acceptable as a first step, but apparently it was now unacceptable. The S.N.P. was pledged to work with the government's proposals, but now the Chairman was saying that only the S.N.P. could deliver the 'National Assembly' to which Scots were entitled. The one-great-leap-to-independence model supposedly had been replaced by the devolutionary-scenic-route model, yet it was now argued that changes in the electorate were making the latter policy redundant almost as soon as it had been adopted. The old policies would not lie down.[30]

It can be argued that it was a reasonable tactic to demand more than the minimum until the government finalised its own proposals, and that it was in the interests of 'strong' devolution to delay these for as long as possible while support for more powers continued to grow. There was evidence to support this view, according to the S.N.P., in a 'Systems Three' survey published in November which showed that 30% of Labour voters were contemplating switching to the S.N.P. if the government gave only minimal economic powers to the assembly.[31] Thus, when the government's White Paper was published in November, it was met by a barrage of criticism from the nationalists.

In a lengthy two-part press statement, George Reid attacked the proposals on two grounds, the first of which was quite predictable, namely that the assembly lacked economic, fiscal and industrial powers. The second was somewhat obscure. It was argued that the retention of veto powers by Westminster undermined Scottish political sovereignty. Described as the most objectionable feature of the White Paper, this seemingly arcane point is in fact far more important to an understanding of the party's attitude to devolution than any considerations of electoral tactics. Central to the devolutionist case within the S.N.P. was support for the idea that sovereignty resided in the Scottish people rather than 'in a parliament at Westminster'. This affirmed the essential nationalist principle which separated the S.N.P. from the 'British' parties. As it was incumbent upon the Scottish people 'to decide when the devolution process should stop', it could be argued that devolution was a 'launching pad' for independence; greater concessions would be won if Scottish public opinion could be persuaded to support them.[32] However, if it was acknowledged that the assembly's right to exist was conditional upon Westminster, then the devolutionist case was weakened, and a reversion to the old 'mandate' strategy became more attractive to opponents and sceptical supporters of devolution alike. This basic difference in philosophy coloured the S.N.P.'s whole attitude to devolution, and it was the failure to come to terms with it which delivered those who supported a pro-devolutionary strategy into the hands of their enemies both inside and outside the party.

In the meantime, the party pledged itself to try to strengthen 'any devolution bill the government eventually brought forward' in the wake of the White Paper, and the 'launch pad' strategy was formally legitimised by an emergency resolution to the December meeting of the National Council. A national campaign was proposed to publicise the S.N.P.'s attitude to the White Paper, and local 'consult the people' initiatives would be carried out to ascertain what powers people thought an assembly should have. Had the party simply stuck to the strategy agreed to by conference by plugging away at its newly found commitment to support any democratically elected assembly however, then neither this campaign nor the subsequent slide away from public opinion need have taken place. The obscure philosophical embellishments over sovereignty were irrelevant to the electorate, and ultimately damaging to the party.

Yet the political climate had never been more favourable for both the S.N.P. and strong devolution. A new O.R.C. poll published in December 1975, showed that support for options (4) and (5) of the April 1974 survey had risen to 49% of those surveyed, and that S.N.P. voters were nudging towards other voters (there had been a slight decrease in the percentage of

S.N.P. voters supporting independence, probably resulting from the rise to 37% of the sample intending to vote S.N.P.). On the other hand, there was also fairly conclusive evidence that the party should pursue a moderate, gradualist strategy: 64% of S.N.P. voters were either very strongly or fairly strongly in favour of the government's assembly plans, compared to 26% of Conservative voters, 40% of Labour voters and 48% of Liberal voters. It was somewhat paradoxical that Labour voters were less enthusiastic about the government's plan than S.N.P. voters were.[33]

These findings could be interpreted in a number of ways of course. It could be that non-S.N.P. voters were more critical of the White Paper because they favoured stronger devolution than S.N.P. voters did, but this hardly accorded with the other data in the survey. On the other hand, it could be that they did not want change at all when actually confronted with it; alternatively, they did not really know what they wanted because devolution did not matter much anyway. What is clear is that the party chose to put the first interpretation on these ambiguous findings, although there was other limited evidence supporting its assessment. A survey published in the *Glasgow Herald* in January showed that 37% of the sample were satisfied and 48% dissatisfied with the White Paper, and of the latter group, 92% wanted 'more powers or complete independence'.[34] Second, in a local government by-election at East Kilbride on 4 February, the party's candidate increased the Nationalist majority six-fold.

This selective reading of the opinion polls coupled with the unenthusiastic reception of the White Paper and a favourable local by-election result conspired to raise expectations and encourage the belief that devolution was undergoing rapid obsolesence. When the White Paper was debated in the Commons in January, Gordon Wilson stated that unless the government increased the powers of the assembly, then the Scottish people would have 'to move on to more certain ways of getting justice'.[35] At the launch of the 'Independence means . . .' leaflet a few days after the East Kilbride result, William Wolfe claimed that Scots were more receptive to the idea of independence than they had been at any time since 1707, and some within the party predicted that Scotland would achieve independence at the next general election. When the National Council met in March, devolution was almost of minor interest. There was even discussion of setting up an alternative government if the 'English' refused to negotiate with an S.N.P. majority at the next election.[36]

Such judgements were premature to say the least. When the next opinion poll appeared (in April), it showed S.N.P. support back at 29%, with Labour ahead on 34%, and by June the party's position had deteriorated further.[37] Unlike the previous favourable poll, however, these surveys were discounted. The party chairman claimed that opinion polls had 'consistently underestimated S.N.P. support' and preferred instead to rely on the party's own 'consult the people' campaign which showed S.N.P. support as high as 56% and not less than 33.5%.[38] The Chairman's public statements were of course predictable and normal reactions by a professional politician to adverse news, but the suspension of belief was not simply a public relations exercise. As noted earlier, good news from whatever source, including the party's own amateur survey efforts, served to reinforce what people wanted to believe anyway, while bad news was generally ignored. Thus, despite the warning signs of the April and June opinion surveys, the party hardened rather than softened its position on devolution.

When the annual conference assembled in May, *The Scotsman* described the conference agenda as a 'draft manifesto for an independent Scotland', and claimed that many activists wanted to fight the next election on the issue of independence.[39] The crucial debate on the devolution strategy was occasioned by Resolution 48 which was jointly sponsored by the National Council and Hamilton-Douglas Branch, and it is worth recalling the exact wording since so much importance has been attached to it subsequently:

Conference reaffirms that independence is the goal of the S.N.P. and, though prepared to accept an assembly with limited powers as a possible stepping stone, asserts that nothing short of independence will meet the needs of the Scottish people in whom alone the sovereign power of Scotland resides.[40]

This was decidedly lukewarm towards devolution when compared to the 1975 decision, and by bringing the question of sovereignty right into the foreground, the party seemed to be saying that concern for doctrinal propriety was greater than the desire for electoral growth. The 1975 conference had endorsed an evolutionary strategy prefaced on an extended process of participation in whatever devolution plans the government brought forward. It had been promised to 'make a constructive contribution' and to 'work vigorously to extend the assembly's powers'. The 1976 resolution said only that the party was 'prepared to accept an assembly with limited powers as a possible stepping stone' to independence, which presumably could well be achieved by other means. The earlier recognition that independence did not yet command majority support was now replaced by the assertion that 'nothing short of independence' would meet Scottish demands, despite the considerable evidence to the contrary.

Yet even this did not go far enough for some delegates. An amendment sponsored jointly by East Kilbride constituency association and Glenrothes branch to delete the phrase 'though prepared to accept an assembly with limited powers as a possible stepping stone' was defeated by 594 votes to 425, which was hardly an overwhelming victory for the moderates in the leadership. It was evident from the conference proceedings that the cautious strategy of the previous year had been abandoned. A widely reported speech by Douglas Henderson (S.N.P. M.P. for Aberdeenshire East), had whipped delegates into a frenzy of nationalist affirmation, and created an undesirable, if not sinister, image of the party. Ironically, this speech has been somewhat charitably interpreted as an attempt to hold the party together in the face of the disagreement over devolution. If this was the only means of uniting the delegates, then it showed just how far the party had stepped back from the 1975 strategy and had returned to a more fundamentalist orientation.

Thus, 1976 did not represent a final and decisive victory for devolution in the S.N.P. On the contrary, it showed just how divided the party had become, and while no direct causal link can be established, the mismanagement of the opportunity created by the 1975 decision must have been a contributory factor. Senior party figures seemed to be unable to grasp the implications of the victory they had achieved, and destroyed their own policy almost as soon as it was adopted through the demands for more powers and the references to the sacred cow of Scottish sovereignty. In the following months, the incumbent leadership attempted to rescue the moderate image so carefully constructed a year earlier, but, as we will show, they were unsuccessful in this venture. Just as they had been the architects of a potentially winning strategy, they were now the victims of their own failure to implement that strategy.

Reclaiming devolution 1976–77

In the wake of the events of Motherwell, the tide of rhetoric went into reverse. Apparently realising that the party's devolution strategy was drifting seriously, the incumbents in the leadership tried to reassure the voters who, they perceived, were alarmed by atavistic nationalism. The idea of an Association of British States (of which nothing had been heard since 1972) was revived in July in a 'retreat' from pure separatism.[41] In his report to the

September meeting of the party's National Council, William Wolfe drew attention the adverse electoral consequence of 'an intransigent posture which it may not be possible to maintain'; rather than frightening the voters, the interests of the party might require some deflation of the expectations of its activists instead:

> We must avoid projecting an aggressive or destructive image. Reassurance is the essence of what we must project . . . it is safer for us to risk provoking impatience among our dedicated supporters than to try to satisfy nationalist sentiment at the risk of alienating possible new support . . . it is more effective . . . to let the electorate get frustrated, then tap their support . . . than to show impatience with the electorate to make apparently excessive and unreasonable demands of the U.K. government.[42]

The remarkable candour of this statement indicated the gravity of the problem that had been created by the party's indulgence of its own preferences at conference and in the public utterances of its spokesmen. These would not impress the electorate favourably, and electoral considerations would have to take precedence over the aspirations of 'dedicated supporters' if the party was to make further progress. But not everyone shared this view. At the same meeting, Margo MacDonald was suggesting that voters 'must be encouraged to make their choice between independence and devolution' in the event of a referendum, as a vote for independence in excess of 30% could be considered a 'moral victory'.[43]

There was no evidence that the moral victory was even attainable. On the contrary, the new O.R.C. survey published in October showed a decline in support for the strong devolution/independence options to 45% from 49%, and an increase in support for the status quo from 14% to 23%. Moreover, if offered a choice between the status quo and independence, 73% of the sample opted to vote for the status quo with only 18% against, and there was only a 1% majority against the status quo among S.N.P. supporters. On the other hand, when voters were asked whether they would vote for or against the 'government going ahead with their plans for a Scottish Assembly', 65% were in favour and only 16% against, with S.N.P. voters making up the most enthusiastic group (87% in favour and 13% against).[44]

The preference for an unattainable moral victory over an achievable real victory was underlined at the November meeting of the National Council. Margo McDonald's report observed that the party's strategy over the last year had been 'to concentrate on the ultimate aim of independence rather than the tactical option of devolution'. Instead of being a preface to some critical remarks, the report added that a campaign of independence 'would be the most enjoyable of the campaigns the S.N.P. has so far engaged in', and would have the great advantage of mobilising the party faithful for action – precisely the opposite effect to that desired by the chairman.[45] In the event, the party in Scotland campaigned around the slogan 'Only Independence Will . . .' for the whole three month life of the Scotland and Wales bill between November 1976 and February 1977.

On the other hand, moderate statements were forthcoming from some of the M.P.s. When the Queen's speech was debated in the House at the end of November, Donald Stewart said that the S.N.P. would support the Scotland and Wales bill, while trying to strengthen the powers available to the assembly, and in the second reading debate he denied that the S.N.P. was intent on wrecking the assembly. George Reid welcomed the bill on the grounds that it represented 'the greatest single transfer of responsibility back to the people of Scotland in 269 years', and was even more anodyne than Mr Stewart, saying that the S.N.P. would not try to strengthen the bill at the risk of causing unnecessary delay in its passage through parliament.[46]

But this has to be placed in the wider context of the party's overall strategy of stressing the virtues of independence, and the weakness of the position of S.N.P. moderates could be easily exposed: even if one accepted that devolution would allow, in Mr Reid's words, for 'gradual progress' towards independence, devolution was still only a means to an end and not an end in itself. There was no consensus in the party that the assembly was intrinsically worthy of its support, as party spokesman obligingly pointed out. For example, Margaret Bain stated during the second reading debate of the Scotland and Wales bill that she had joined the S.N.P. to work for 'the independence of my country' and not for devolution, and Gordon Wilson said that as the purpose of the S.N.P. was to obtain independence for Scotland, the Scotland and Wales bill was a 'temporary expedient'.[47] Unionist opponents of the S.N.P. and devolution alike really had to do very little when party spokesmen were making statements like this. Thus, despite the efforts to return to the 1975 position, anti-devolutionary opinion was crystallising, and there was now an evident lack of cohesion within the leadership on the issue.

The disjuncture between public opinion and party policy was growing simultaneously. Over the same period as the 'Only Independence Will . . .' campaign was running, support for the strong devolution/independence options had slipped from 45% to 40%, and only a minority (43%) of S.N.P. supporters now favoured complete independence.[48] Yet less than a week after this new survey was published, the parliamentary group tabled an amendment to the Scotland and Wales bill for the inclusion of a referendum on independence. When the timetable motion for the Scotland and Wales bill was lost, so terminating the government's plans, it was reported that there was a clamour within the S.N.P. to bring the government down, although the attitude of the M.P.s was equivocal.[49] The result was a joint decision taken by the N.E.C. and the parliamentary group on 1 March to sponsor a new bill to establish a Scottish assembly which would work out its own powers once the first elections to it had been held. Described by George Reid as 'a reasonable way out of the parliamentary log-jam',[50] it was an open-ended commitment which the government was bound to reject, as its architects must have realised.

However, it is better interpreted as a rearguard action by those within the leadership who were trying to reclaim devolution for the party, but who were losing the battle. The party in Scotland had long since abandoned devolution as a priority. As noted above, Margo McDonald had reported in November 1976 that the party had been concentrating on the independence message for a year, and in her report to the March 1977 meeting of the National Council, she restated her view that this was tactically sound and should therefore be continued in party's spring campaign. Thus, at the campaigning level, independence had been a priority over devolution for sixteen months and would continue to be so, no matter what the M.P.s had been saying and in spite of Mr Wolfe's and others' post-conference supplications. Whatever else this might have been, it certainly could not be described as a 'strategy'.

According to the polls, the failure of the Scotland and Wales bill did no harm to the S.N.P.'s ratings in the short term. There was a reversal of its decline in surveys conducted in March and April, and thus the party performed well in the local government elections (for district councils) in May, gaining over 100 seats. In one sense, this was another misfortune for constitutional 'moderates' within the leadership, as it encouraged the party to press ahead with its independence theme and precluded participation in the newly-formed all-party Alliance for a Scottish Assembly. A 'mini-referendum' had been conducted in five constituencies at the end of March, and the party claimed that the results showed to within an accuracy of 5% that 50% of voters now favoured independence.[51] The reliability of these data was highly questionable in the context of the decline in support for the strong devolution/independence options in surveys conducted before the Scotland and Wales bill fiasco, and the evident stagnation if not decline in party membership noted by the party Treasurer in his report to the March meeting of the National Council.

Nevertheless, the mini-referendum and the gains made by the S.N.P. at the expense of Labour in the local government elections did nothing to strengthen the devolutionist case within the party. The parliamentary group refused an invitation from Michael Foot, the minister with overall responsibility for devolution, to discuss the issue and declared that the government could not expect the S.N.P. to maintain it in power in exchange for a new bill. In the run up to the annual conference in May, press reports noted that independence would be the main theme, and that devolution was not even scheduled for discussion.[52]

In summary, the attempt to reclaim devolution was a failure. Neither the fact that support for strong devolution and independence was ebbing, even among the party's own supporters, nor the signs of organisational stagnation made much overall impression on strategy. The party's campaigning effort in Scotland was geared towards independence, and there was an underlying scepticism about devolution which was difficult to suppress. Unable to abide by the strategy which it had constructed for itself in 1975, the party leadership was showing signs of fragmentation as individuals took up conflicting positions in what seemed like a policy free-for-all. It must be said that events at Westminster must have made even the most enthusiastic devolutionists cynical, and that the government was in perhaps greater disarray than the S.N.P. Nevertheless, it had managed to put itself in a moderate position at the outset, and the S.N.P. had not succeeded in dislodging it from there. Not possessing the advantages of office and long-standing voter loyalty, the S.N.P. could afford to make fewer mistakes than its rivals.

Policy disintegration and organisational crisis

The proceedings of the S.N.P.'s 1977 conference reflected its advance billing, as delegates and platform speakers alike affirmed the policy of 'Independence – Nothing Less'. In adopting this new hard line, the parliamentary group placed itself in an absurd position; it would support a new devolution bill, but it would also seek to bring the government down at the first opportunity.[53] If it was in earnest about supporting a new devolution bill, then it had to sustain the government in office, as the party's constitutional expert, Neil MacCormick, had already pointed out. On the other hand, if it really meant to vote the government out of office at the first opportunity then it could not be very serious about a new devolution bill. Any new initiative from the government would rapidly expose the S.N.P.'s lack of credible strategy, and it did not take long before this happened.

When the government announced in July that it would bring forth new legislative proposals, Donald Stewart said that the parliamentary group would adopt a 'wait and see' approach to see if they were any better than the previous ones; if this was the case, he said that he thought that it was 'quite likely that the S.N.P. would back (them)'.[54] Thus, despite the conference rhetoric, the exorcism of devolution now appeared little more than a ritual, and when asked what the S.N.P. would do if asked to support the government, the party's devolution spokesman, George Reid, circumspectly admitted that there was a trade-off, as Neil MacCormick had suggested:

> If the present administration is serious about its devolution objectives, it will have the support of the S.N.P. on that measure alone. On any vote of confidence, the S.N.P. will decide how to vote on how the Scottish promises bear up to the reality of the progress made in returning decision making to the Scottish people.[55]

As may have been expected, the fudging and 'instant policy making' endemic to a Westminster without a reliable government majority was not necessarily understood in Edinburgh. The party was not used to parliamentary representation let alone influence on the government itself, and a 'summit' between William Wolfe and Donald Stewart took place in July in order to improve working relationships between the M.P.s and the leadership in Scotland. It was decided to set up a joint N.E.C./parliamentary group working party which would define 'clear lines of communication, consultation and responsibility', because the party 'had to get accustomed to the existence of our parliamentary group', and it in turn had to reach an understanding with the party.[56] This meeting tends to support the view that the creation of a parliamentary group had bifurcated the leadership structure, as it can be deduced from Mr Wolfe's comments that relationships were less than perfect and had caused concern for some time. However, what was an organisational problem only became a crisis when there was open disagreement in the party, and this was not apparent yet.

The party was indeed beset by organisational difficulties elsewhere, as there was persistent concern over the stagnation of party membership and the adverse effect it was having on party finances throughout the remainder of the year; moreover, the difficulties with the devolution policy worsened when the Scotland bill came before Parliament in the autumn. On the basis of their previous experience, there was no conviction among the M.P.s that they would be able to make any real improvements to the bill. Gordon Wilson described the bill as 'not . . . particularly good but . . . the best we are likely to get'.[57] Yet, the S.N.P. group tabled amendments to it regardless of the certainty of failure, or of their effect in slowing the bill's progress. The reason for this was almost certainly pressure from the party in Scotland which continued to make quite unrealistic demands.

Following the December meeting of the National Council for example, William Wolfe repeated the demand that a question on independence be included in the devolution referendum, as a 20% vote would 'be a moral victory for the S.N.P.'[58] This argument it will be recalled, had already been advanced by Margo MacDonald, although interestingly the price of moral victory had fallen from 30% to 20%, perhaps as a concession to realism. In fact, Mr Wolfe's demand has to be placed in the wider context of opinion within the National Council, against which it looked quite moderate and perhaps even an attempt to salvage a bit of a pro-devolutionary strategy. An attempt was made at the same meeting to reject Margo MacDonald's report because it only urged campaigning for independence in the context of a 'yes' vote for devolution; some of the delegates wanted the party to withdraw from campaigning completely, or to register a 'no' vote for devolution if a question on independence were not included in the referendum (as indeed some of them did).

Moving amendments in parliament gave the impression that the M.P.s were achieving something. Thus, Gordon Wilson reported to the National Council that the group had succeeded in improving the bill despite the fact that all the S.N.P. amendments had been defeated and the assembly lacked the powers the party wanted for it. When the committee stage resumed in the new year, the group tabled yet more amendments (on taxation and industrial powers, an independence referendum, and proportional representation), all of which were lost, but all of which were duly reported to party organisations in the parliamentary group's 'Contact' magazine.[59] The problem for the group was that a huge credibility gap appeared when it was really tested. The so-called 'Cunningham amendment' which proposed that at least 40% of registered Scottish voters must vote 'yes' in order that the assembly be set up was a case in point. The S.N.P. M.P.s were naturally extremely hostile to this unprecedented proposal, but nevertheless had to accept it and continue to support the government to ensure the passage of the bill. This was not popular among some sections of the party in Scotland.[60]

The party's poor showing at the parliamentary by-election at Glasgow Garscadden in April has to be seen in the context of this increasing disarray over devolution. Although there were local factors which made the S.N.P. vulnerable – in particular its failure to support shipbuilding nationalisation – the party's inability to capitalise on its own strengths and the weaknesses of the incumbent (Labour) party was symptomatic of a wider malaise. The S.N.P. tried to avoid devolution completely by making the government's record on unemployment the main issue. Donald Dewar, the Labour candidate, under no obligation to accept the S.N.P.'s definition of political discourse in Garscadden, switched the attack onto the party's policy on devolution instead and put the S.N.P. on the defensive for the rest of the campaign. This should not have happened. Shortly after campaigning began in earnest, the S.N.P. was presented with a new propaganda weapon in the form of the Cunningham amendment to the Scotland bill which gave substance to the party's claim that Labour could not be trusted with devolution, especially if it retained Garscadden.

The S.N.P. had the opportunity to re-enter the debate as the only reliable supporter of devolution if it could test Labour's sincerity in the newly-formed 'Yes for Scotland' coalition for devolution. Yet the party failed to take this advantage, and seemed intent instead on marginalising itself. At a meeting of the National Council in Paisley (only a few miles from Garscadden) on 4 March, Gordon Wilson actually recommended that party members should 'not speak on the same platform as people who are normally our opponents' when the devolution referendum campaign got under way.[61] This hardly gave the impression that the party was willing to make common cause in the overriding interest of the establishment of a Scottish assembly. Worse was to follow however. On March 14, the party announced the impending publication of its policies for an independent Scotland and an official press release of 21 March stated that the party's 'prime objective . . . to regain independence for Scotland' was the same now as it had been when the National Party of Scotland was formed in 1928.[62]

Thus the Labour candidate could say with some justification that his S.N.P. opponent was 'showing quite extraordinary cheek in claiming that independence would not be an issue in the April 13 election' when members of his own party continued to make it an issue.[63] An 'exit' poll of 3,000 Garscadden voters showed the failure of the S.N.P.'s campaign, as voters had not connected the unemployment issue (on which Labour was strong), with the

Scottish issues of devolution and oil (on which the S.N.P. was strong).[64] Instead of challenging the government's questionable commitment to devolution and attacking its failure to carry many of its own supporters as matters of the highest priority, the S.N.P. tried to fight the government on an issue on which it was strong and allowed itself to be isolated on the constitutional question. Labour held Garscadden with a increased majority of over 4,000, as the S.N.P.'s vulnerability in a key policy area began to affect what had been generally considered as a vibrant and dynamic capacity for electioneering at the constituency level.

Encouraged by this result, the government moved the writ shortly afterwards for the Hamilton by-election, a seat which the S.N.P. had won in 1967. There was further proof of a Labour recovery in Scotland in the Regional Council elections in May, and a Systems Three survey published on May 12 showed that 47% of the sample intended to vote Labour, while S.N.P. support was down to 24%.[65] Some elements in the party leadership evidently were able to respond to these setbacks. In an apparent reversal of tactics, devolution was made the centrepiece of the S.N.P.'s campaign at Hamilton, with the government's shaky commitment being fully exploited. The party's candidate (Margo MacDonald) endorsed the assembly plans and announced that the S.N.P. parliamentary group would be supporting the government's closure motion on the Scotland bill. However, these tactics did not meet with universal approval. The recently defeated campaigners in the Garscadden Constituency Association were urging the leadership to go in the opposite direction by hardening the party line on independence.

Thus, the party assembled for its annual conference in a state of pessimism and some confusion, although, because of the impending by-election, disagreements between traditionalists and gradualists were muted. There was no specifically designated debate on devolution, as there were no new proposals on either devolution or the referendum. Even so, an 'underlying but fundamental' divide could be perceived according to some press reports. The accuracy of this assessment was confirmed once the by-election was over. It was reported that critics of the party leadership would try to force the party to abandon devolution once and for all, despite the reasonable performance at Hamilton.[66] When the National Council met in Dunblane on 10 June, the Chairman's report put the case for supporting devolution. It argued that the party's poor performance was attributable to a number of factors, but that two of the most significant were the government's commitment to devolution and public hostility to independence.

The implication was that the party should give a general commitment to support the government, and at the same time build a coalition of all those 'committed to S.N.P. aims' (this referred to the new Scottish Labour Party and other sympathetic devolutionists) through the proposed campaign 'The Democratic Road to Self-Government'.[67]

The case for an adversarial strategy was contained in a resolution sponsored by Alex Ewing and William Steven which called on the National Council 'to campaign for a "No" vote in the devolution referendum and reaffirm the slogan "Independence – Nothing Less".'[68] It was clear that there was substantial support for this position, so instead of forcing a confrontation in a straight vote, an amendment substituting the word 'Yes' for 'No' was proposed and carried, and the resolution was then passed. This did not reverse the spirit of the resolution however, and the party was now committed to campaign for an assembly which it rejected on the principle of 'Independence – Nothing Less'. Such an absurd policy did nothing to enhance the party's credibility, and when the next opinion survey was published, it showed S.N.P. support down to 20%, a level which was maintained throughout the summer.[69]

It appears then that the critics of devolution within the party were growing more active and vociferous despite increasingly strong evidence that the 'Independence – Nothing Less' policy advocated as an alternative would result in nothing except electoral oblivion. But with the effective collapse of the devolution policy, it was not difficult to see that the anti-devolutionists were filling a rapidly expanding policy vacuum. This process was hastened by a renewed crisis in the parliamentary strategy (or lack of strategy), which had now entered its most serious phase. In an official party press release dated July 17, Neil MacCormick, the party's constitutional expert, restated his view that the party must support the government until the referendum had taken place. In the following few days, reports appeared in the press that the parliamentary group would not support such a deal, and that there was a rift between the group and party leaders in Scotland. The idea of any formal pact between the government and the S.N.P. seems to have been finally rejected at the beginning of August, and the decision was affirmed by the N.E.C. and the National Council in September.[70]

The problem was that no alternative strategy had been agreed upon, so that when parliament reassembled in the autumn, the parliamentary group was still divided over whether to oppose the Queen's speech or not. To make matters worse, this was being exacerbated by lobbying from other sources within the party.

Douglas Henderson had fired a warning shot in their direction at the end of September saying that while the group 'welcomes advice and consultation from party candidates, office bearers, the executive committee and so forth . . . it will itself as a group make a decision'.[71] According to reports at the end of October and beginning of November, Donald Stewart and Hamish Watt had indicated that they would support the government in the vote on the Queen's speech and the group had been instructed by the N.E.C. not to bring the government down until March (the date of the referendum).

However, in the debate on the Queen's speech, Margaret Bain cast doubt on this. It appeared that at least three of the M.P.s had refused to back the government, and it was reported in *The Scotsman* on 9 November that the parliamentary group had rejected the N.E.C.'s instructions altogether, and would vote against the government; when the vote took place, George Reid and Hamish Watt broke ranks by not voting against the government (Mr Reid voted with the government and Mr Watt abstained), and they were both disciplined by the group.

Thus, the parliamentary group had asserted its authority over the party by disciplining two of its number who had sought to follow the instructions of the party's own executive. In turn, the parliamentary group earned a rebuke from senior officials for voting with the Conservatives, who only a month before had decided to campaign against devolution. The press release issued by party headquarters in Edinburgh following the Queen's speech came from George Reid rather than the nine M.P.s who had voted against the government, and although it purported to express a personal view only, it undoubtedly reflected majority sentiment among the non-parliamentary members of the N.E.C. Relationships between the M.P.s and the executive were now worse than ever despite the 'machinery' set up in 1977 to improve them. In his valediction as party chairman a few days after these events, William Wolfe alluded to the unsatisfactory relationships which had produced this chaotic series of decisions. While he favoured the emphasis of 'the party leadership remaining in Scotland', his own guidelines were still unclear in their allocation of responsibility.[72]

It is clear then that the party had not resolved the structural and executive problems resulting from the creation of a parliamentary group, and that these had intensified under the pressures of a highly divisive issue. Devolution was acting as a solvent on the new and fragile bonds between a vigorous party leadership and a novice parliamentary party. However, it would be erroneous to attribute all the weaknesses of the devolution strategy to this problematic relationship. The deliberations of the party's National Assembly in October indicated a more general rift. The discussion centred around the document 'A General Strategy for an Assembly manifesto' which restated the basic position agreed by the 1975 conference; this time around however, there was no agreement, let alone a decisive majority in favour, and the sections approving the government's assembly and referendum plans were remitted for rewording.[73]

Nor were organisational problems confined to the relationship between the executive and the parliamentary group. First, there was open conflict between the N.E.C. and the Berwick and East Lothian constitutency association over candidate selection for the by-election in October. The association had chosen William Patterson as its prospective candidate, but he failed to get the endorsement of the N.E.C., which chose one of its own members, Isobel Lindsay, to replace him. Patterson, with the support of some of the constituency association members, then campaigned against Miss Lindsay during the by-election, and the S.N.P. finished a poor third. Patterson was expelled from the party on 3 November, and when the National Council met in December delegates were issued with an N.E.C. document of unprecedented length (five pages), setting out the executive's account of events. There were additional reports from the National Secretary and the Executive Vice-Chairman for organisation, a statement from the Berwick dissidents and printed extracts from the party constitution. Considering that a referendum was shortly to be held to decide whether or not an elected assembly for Scotland should be set up, the pre-occupation with the Berwick affair was an astounding comment on the party's priorities, and as the party Chairman observed, 'did nothing for our credibility'. Secondly, the Treasurer's report to the December meeting showed a rapid fall in the sale of membership cards resulting in a sharp deterioration in the financial situation of party headquarters, and consequently in its ability to mount any effective campaign.[74]

Thus, by the end of 1978, the party was in a lamentable condition. At the organisation level, the leadership lacked cohesion and had effectively broken down; the parliamentary group was in a state of confusion, at odds with itself and with other members of the executive, and the party was diminished in strength in the localities. At the policy level, the devolution strategy had long since broken down, despite repeated attempts and opportunities to rescue it, as the party had retreated towards 'Independence – Nothing Less'. Not only did the party make no real effort to construct a coalition around a pro-devolutionary policy in the first place (which was perhaps understandable in the light of its hesitancy over the issue generally), but it failed to take the opportunities it did have to enter such coalitions at an early stage. This self-imposed marginalisation had benefited the party's opponents, with Labour consolidating itself as the party of devolution, and the Conservatives aligning with those who opposed constitutional change, so turning the referendum increasingly into a familiar contest between the major parties. We shall review the S.N.P.'s role in this contest briefly in the next chapter in the context of the party's retreat into factional politics; what we have shown here is that the ground was already well prepared for retrenchment and a lack-lustre performance in the referendum.

Conclusion

Having achieved a position of real influence for the first time in its history, the S.N.P. was unable to excoriate its independence dogma in the interests of constitutional reform and further political advance. Despite a series of good opportunities engineered by both the incumbent party leadership and the disarray of the government, the party did not establish itself as the principal credible party of devolution. The efforts that were made to move towards the devolutionary mean of public opinion were lost in a continual welter of unrealistic expectations, misjudgements and growing internal dissention. It seems to confirm Luebbert's argument, as the closer the party got to achieving its objective, the greater the disagreement and conflict generated by the detailed proposals emanating from the government. What tended to be lost in the internal debate was the fact that for all their shortcomings, the government's devolution proposals did indeed represent, in George Reid's words, 'The greatest single transfer of responsibility back to the people of Scotland in 269 years'.

As we have suggested, it was perhaps unfortunate that the incumbents in the party leadership failed to get elected to parliament in 1974 as this may have obviated some of the organisational tensions that did arise. Yet the fact that there were no guidelines to deal with the eventuality of a parliamentary group (the creation of which was being predicted by the party itself in 1974), showed either a lack of planning and forethought, or the lack of a consensus about what such a group should do, or both. Thus, the turmoil created by devolution only revealed organisational and doctrinal conflicts and weaknesses that were already present. It was not that the party was less centralised in 1978 than it was in 1974, but rather that the leadership was incoherent where it had been coherent.

It is apparent that the party's overriding goals were still important influences on the decision makers throughout the period. These tended to cloud judgements about the objective state of public opinion for example, and were still discernible beneath the pro-devolutionary policy which did exist. Thus, devolution was never accorded any intrinsic merit other than its contributory function of facilitating national sovereignty. Whether it stemmed from genuine conviction or from pragmatic concessions to their party opponents, this doctrinal approach to devolution put the pro-devolutionists within the leadership into a weak position, and it was exploited by internal and external foe alike. It was tempting and easy to alternate between support for devolution and independence when opponents of the leadership could mobilise party opinion behind the basic policy of independence for Scotland at the annual conference, the National Council and the National Assembly. While this may have guaranteed the incumbents continuing popularity at these events (and in the voting that took place at them), it did nothing to enhance the image of competence and moderation which the leadership was trying to construct in the wider electoral arena.

Notes

[1] Constitution of the Scottish National Party, 1948, in Brand, *The National Movement in Scotland*, appendix B, p. 305.

[2] See Miller, *The End of British Politics?*, pp. 99–101.

[3] G. Luebbert, 'A theory of government formation', *Comparative Political Studies* 17, 2, 1984, p. 237.

[4] See, for example, J. Mercer, *Scotland: The Devolution of Power*, London, Calder, 1978, p. 172; Mullin, 'The Scottish National Party;' McAllister, *U.K. Nationalism*, p. 5; Mishler and Mughan, 'Representing the Celtic Fringe' p. 399.

[5] J. G. Kellas, 'Devolution in British Politics', paper delivered to the Political Studies Association, Nottingham, 22–24 March 1976, p. 2; see also H. Drucker and G. Brown, *The Politics of Nationalism and Devolution*, London, Longman, 1980, pp. 80–85; and W. Miller, *What was the profit from following the crowd? The effectiveness of party strategy on immigration and devolution*, Glasgow, Centre for the Study of Public Policy, 1979.

[6] Paper submitted to the National Assembly by Cameron Aitkin, 17 October 1971, Scottish National Party, Edinburgh.

[7] See resolution 31 to the 38th Annual Conference, 27 May 1972, Scottish National

Party, Edinburgh, 1972 and minutes of the National Assembly, ref. NA 73/7, Scottish National Party, Edinburgh, 28 January 1973.

8   Pre-election campaign: Oil and self-government, National Council document to September meeting of the National Council, Scottish National Party, Edinburgh, July 1973.

9   Press releases 7 March 1974 and 4 April 1974, Scottish National Party, Edinburgh.

10   Chairman's report to the National Council, Scottish National Party, Edinburgh, 20 April 1974.

11   See reports in the *Glasgow Herald*, 1 June 1974, *The Scotsman*, 1 June 1974, and *The Guardian*, 1 June 1974.

12   Chairman's report to the National Council, Scottish National Party, Edinburgh, 15 June 1974.

13   See report in *The Scotsman*, 13 May 1974.

14   Chairman's report to the National Council, Scottish National Party, Edinburgh, 15 June 1974.

15   H. C. Debs., vol. 878, cols. 274–275, 29 July 1974.

16   See The Royal Commission on the Constitution, 1968–73, Cmnd. 5460, London. H.M.S.O. and Privy Council Office, *Devolution within the U.K.: Some Alternatives*, London, H.M.S.O., 1974.

17   J. Barry Jones and M. Keating, 'The Labour Party's devolution policy', *Government and Opposition* 17, 3, 1982, pp. 279–292; Miller, *What was the profit in following the crowd?*; Miller, *The End of British Politics?*, p. 259; Drucker and Brown, *The Politics of Nationalism and Devolution*.

18   See report in *The Scotsman*, 4 October 1974.

19   Miller, *The End of British Politics?*, p. 122.

20   See press releases 7 October 1974, 9 October 1974 and 14 October 1974. Scottish National Party, Edinburgh.

21   Chairman's report to the National Council, Scottish National Party, Edinburgh, 7 December 1974, and report by the executive vice-chairman for policy to the National Council, Scottish National Party, Edinburgh, 7 December 1974.

22   National Assembly meeting agenda, appendix 3, Scottish National Party, Edinburgh, 18 January 1975.

23   Report by the executive vice-chairman to the National Council, Scottish National Party, Edinburgh, 1 March 1975.

24   Agenda to the 41st annual conference, 30 May 1975, Scottish National Party, Edinburgh, 1975.

25   See report in the *Glasgow Herald*, 29 May 1975.

26   The actual voting figures were 423–191 against a remit. It is interesting that 1976 rather than 1975 was generally regarded as the turning point for the devolution policy (in so far as any turning point was perceived at all), by those interviewed in 1982.

27   See report in *The Scotsman*, 3 June 1975.

28   See press release no. 212, 17 July 1975, Scottish National Party, Edinburgh, H.C. Debs. vol. 896, col. 2287–89, 31 July 1975, and press release, 1 August 1975, Scottish National Party, Edinburgh.

29   See press release, 30 September 1975, Scottish National Party, Edinburgh and Chairman's report to the National Council, Scottish National Party, Edinburgh, 6 September 1975.

30   Isobel Lindsay remarked that the party had been 'living off the policy work carried out in the late 1960s together with instant policy making', report by the executive vice-chairman for publicity to the National Council, Scottish National Party, Edinburgh, 6 September 1975.

31   See press release, 17 November 1975, Scottish National Party, Edinburgh.

32   See press release, 27 November 1975, Scottish National Party, Edinburgh.

[33] See report in *The Scotsman*, 16 December 1975; Miller notes that there was a decline in S.N.P. support in the opinion polls throughout 1975, but that there was leap 'to a peak of 37% in December in response to the government's so-called 'colonial' white paper on devolution', Miller, *The End of British Politics?*, p. 231.

[34] See report in the *Glasgow Herald*, 19 January 1976.

[35] H.C. Debs. vol. 903, col. 1038, 19 January 1976.

[36] Minute of the National Council ref. NC 76/9, 6 March 1976.

[37] See report in the *Glasgow Herald*, 12 April 1976.

[38] See report in the *Glasgow Herald*, 14 June 1975, and see minute of the National Council ref. NC 76/25, Scottish National Party, Edinburgh, 12 June 1976.

[39] See report in *The Scotsman*, 13 May 1976.

[40] Agenda to the 42nd annual conference, resolution 48, 29 May 1976, Scottish National Party, Edinburgh, 1976.

[41] See reports in the *The Times*, 4 June 1976 and 21 July 1976, *The Scotsman*, 21 July 1976, and the *Glasgow Herald*, 25 July 1976.

[42] Chairman's report to the National Council, Scottish National Party, Edinburgh, 4 September 1976.

[43] Minutes of the National Council, ref. NC 76/50, Scottish National Party, Edinburgh, 4 September 1976.

[44] See report in *The Scotsman*, 28 October 1976.

[45] Report by the executive vice-chairman for policy to the National Council, National Council minute ref. NC 76/74, Scottish National Party, Edinburgh, 6 November 1976.

[46] H.C. Debs. vol. 922, col. 1354, 14 December 1976.

[47] H.C. Debs. vol. 924, cols. 491–492, 19 January 1977.

[48] See report in *The Scotsman*, 9 February 1977.

[49] See reports in the *Glasgow Herald*, 28 February 1977, and *The Times*, 24 February 1977.

[50] See press release, 1 March 1977 and see report in *The Scotsman*, 2 March 1977.

[51] See report in the *Glasgow Herald*, 5 April 1977. The independence question in the 'survey' did not actually mention the word 'independence', but referred to a 'Scottish parliament within the Commonwealth, with full powers, with Queen as Head of State'.

[52] See reports in the *Glasgow Herald*, *The Times* and *The Scotsman*, 10 May 1977.

[53] See reports in the *Glasgow Herald*, *The Guardian* and *The Scotsman*, 26 May 1977, *The Guardian* and *The Scotsman*, 27 May 1977, and *The Sunday Times*, 29 May 1977.

[54] See report in the *Glasgow Herald*, 15 July 1977. Neil McCormick's restatement of the gradualist case was made in *The Times*, 17 May 1977.

[55] See press releases of 26 and 27 July 1977, Scottish National Party, Edinburgh and report in the *Glasgow Herald*, 28 July 1977.

[56] See press release 21 July 1977, Scottish National Party, Edinburgh.

[57] H.C. Debs. vol. 939, col. 623, 16 November 1977.

[58] See press release 5 December 1977, Scottish National Party, Edinburgh.

[59] See H.C. Debs, vol. 941, col. 1573 10 January 1978, and vol. 942, col. 410, 17 January 1978, and see press release 23 January 1978, Scottish National Party, Edinburgh.

[60] According to a report in the *Glasgow Herald*, the Glasgow Cathcart constituency association had called upon the M.P.s to withdraw support from the Scotland Bill after the passage of the Cunningham amendment. See report in the *Glasgow Herald*, 18 February 1978.

[61] For Gordon Wilson's comments, see minutes of the National Council ref. NC

78/13, Scottish National Party, Edinburgh, 3 March 1978. The leading instigator of the 'Yes for Scotland' campaign, launched in January 1978, was John P. MacKintosh, Labour M.P. for Berwick and East Lothian. Macartney (1979) argues that YFS failed to attract all-party support because it had no non-nationalist leaders following MacKintosh's death in the summer of 1978. He also argues that if the S.N.P. had joined the YFS forerunner (Alliance for a Scottish Assembly), then the possibility of an all-party devolution coalition would have been better. See A. Macartney, 'The protagonists', ch. 2 in J. Bochel, D. Denver and A. Macartney (eds.), *The Referendum Experience: Scotland 1979*, Aberdeen, Aberdeen University Press, 1979.

[62] See press release, 21 March 1978, Scottish National Party, Edinburgh.

[63] See reports in the *Glasgow Herald*, 25 March 1978, and the *Evening Times*, 22 March 1978.

[64] See report in *The Sunday Times*, 16 April 1978.

[65] See report in the *Glasgow Herald*, 12 May 1978.

[66] See reports in *The Guardian*, 26 May 1978, and 2 June 1978. The party's candidate secured 34% of the poll at Hamilton.

[67] Chairman's report to the National Council, Scottish National Party, Edinburgh, 10 June 1978.

[68] Minutes of the National Council ref. NC 78/31, Scottish National Party, Edinburgh, 10 June 1978.

[69] See reports in the *Glasgow Herald*, 12 June 1978, 12 July 1978, 14 August 1978 and 11 September 1978.

[70] Minutes of the National Council ref. NC 78/48, Scottish National Party, Edinburgh, 2 September 1978; see report in *The Scotsman*, 9 September 1978, and see earlier reports in *The Guardian*, 18 and 19 July 1978, and in *The Scotsman*, 18 and 22 July 1978.

[71] See press release, 23 September 1978, Scottish National Party, Edinburgh.

[72] The text reads, 'The S.N.P. is still learning how to cope with Westminister representation . . . there must be complementary roles in parliament and in Scotland with the emphasis on the party leadership remaining in Scotland . . . the M.P.s (have) to be responsible for their own tactics in Westminister but consulting with the party when necessary . . . The N.E.C. for its part has to feel free to give advice as it seems fit to the party's M.P.s'. Press release, 14 November 1978, Scottish National Party, Edinburgh.

[73] Minutes of the National Assembly ref. NA 87/24, Scottish National Party, Edinburgh, 15 October 1978.

[74] Minutes of the National Council ref. NC 78/59, Scottish National Party, Edinburgh, 2 December 1978, and Treasurer's report to the National Council, Scottish National Party, Edinburgh, 2 December 1978.

CHAPTER 5

The Descent into Factional Politics

In the run-up to the 1979 Scotland Act referendum, the party was in the worst state it had been for a decade. Having reached a plateau in its growth cycle, it was now in a state of organisational stagnation and electoral downturn. The devolution policy was in complete disarray, membership was declining and the party leadership was immobilised by internal dissension. Effectively fragmented into contender factions, the leadership now had difficulty in performing the most basic and elementary functions within the party. On the strategic level, the party had got increasingly out of touch with public opinion mainly, although not exclusively, through its own efforts, as pragmatic vote winning strategies had given way to more ideological policies. In effect, the S.N.P. was at the point of visible decline.

The question now was how the party would react to these negative developments. There were two possibilities. As on some previous occasions, the leadership could have attempted the recovery of some more electorally popular position at the cost of some internal upheaval. However, such strategies had never proved to be particularly successful even under more favourable conditions. They stood even less chance of success in circumstances where the leadership itself was in pieces. Even if such a strategy could be attempted, there may have been very little perceived electoral pay-off in the prevailing political climate. It was far more likely that there would be an acceleration in the competitive and degenerative processes once the safety valve of growth had been removed. The likely consequences were an increase in leadership turnover, a displacement of incumbents in an intensifying dissension over policy, a further decline in party membership and income and a continuing drift away from public opinion towards the politics of faction.

The party's performance in the referendum and election campaigns of 1979 will be reviewed in the context of these two possibilities. We will then turn to the process of internal debate which took place between 1979 and 1982. Whatever the situation in early 1979, there can be little dispute that the party entered a rapid spiral of decline thenceforth. Incapable of making a rational (market led) appraisal of its failures in this period, it entered a phase of its development in which external strategies became merely adjuncts of internal rivalries. The slide into conflict was such that, by almost every indicator, the party was in a poorer condition in 1982 than it had been in 1972.

The referendum and election campaigns

On the surface, the S.N.P. worked for the 'Yes' side in the referendum campaign. Bochel and Denver's study of the constituency parties shows that 97% of the S.N.P. sample worked for the 'Yes' campaign.[1] Yet Macartney's (1981) assertion that the independence hardliners in the party 'lost the argument quite conclusively' in the lead-in to the referendum on the Scotland Act proposals, is fundamentally wrong.[2] As we have shown, it was the party's devolution policy which was never conclusively resolved. Disagreement on this issue intensified rather than diminished as the referendum approached, and this was reflected during the campaign.

The party's 'unanimous' participation in the referendum campaign must be seen in the context of the decision to let each constituency association choose whether to participate in the 'Yes For Scotland' (YFS) umbrella campaign or run its own.[3] This was no mere technicality. Macartney's own study of campaign themes shows a fairly major difference between official S.N.P. press releases, and those of the Yes For Scotland (YFS) and Labour Movement Yes (LMY) campaigns. While the S.N.P. made eight references to devolution giving 'more Scottish control/influence', neither of the other two campaigns mentioned this at all. Similarly, the S.N.P.'s main leaflet said that the proposed assembly would 'mean self-government over certain areas of Scottish life', while the YFS leaflets made no reference to self-government and stressed that the referendum was about devolution and not separatism.[4] In other words, the S.N.P. material viewed devolution from an independence perspective while the YFS/LMY material viewed it from a unionist perspective.

Given the internal upheavals which had been caused be devolution, it is not difficult to see why many S.N.P. constituency associations must have found it more acceptable to run their own campaigns than to participate in the umbrella organisations. The party leadership obviously did not feel confident enough to impose instructions on local associations; even most of the S.N.P.'s fund raising for the referendum was left to local parties rather than being disbursed centrally.[5] After the referendum was over, it became clear that there had been a wide variation in both the level of local campaigning and in the type of material used. When the National Council met on 3 March in Dundee, the report by the executive vice-chairman for organisation noted that some constituency associations and branches had not campaigned at all, and he suggested that the reason for this had been political rather than organisational.[6] Taken in conjunction with the evident divisions in the leadership, the party had been divided over the issue from top to bottom.

The S.N.P. was not the only party which was divided over devolution, nor perhaps was it the most divided. The problem for the 'Yes' side was that bitter inter-party rivalries – particularly between the S.N.P. and Labour – had to be added to the effects of internal divisions within the S.N.P. Perman (1980) notes that as the 'Yes' side was 'hopelessly divided and its arguments and its efforts were often contradictory', it was an easy target for the 'No' campaigners.[7] If the S.N.P.'s intention was to build an issue coalition through the YFS umbrella group, then it should have joined the Alliance for a Scottish Assembly at the outset (in 1977), taken a radically different attitute to the Labour government in the vote of confidence in the previous autumn and not persisted in making independence its principal campaign theme while criticising the government's devolution proposals. This may have precluded the formation of LMY and guaranteed wider participation in YFS, but it was too late once a background of hostility and policy difference had built up which hindered cooperation.[8]

The S.N.P.'s own referendum campaign continued to criticise the assembly plans, although this was certainly not the sole theme of the party's propaganda as Macartney's analysis shows.[9] William Wolfe pledged 100% support for a yes vote at the campaign launch on 11 January 1979. While he was still censorious of the assembly's lack of powers, he argued that there were seven good reasons why people should vote in favour, as the assembly would be the first step in building a more open and responsive government in Scotland.[10] The party leadership attempted to co-ordinate the S.N.P. effort as far as was possible within the agreed framework of devolved campaigning, and held a special one day conference on devolution at Perth on 20 January.

Described by the *Glasgow Herald* as the dullest in the party's history, it reiterated the call for more powers for the assembly.[11]

The emphasis on new powers tended to fade rapidly however, as the opinion polls showed a steady decline in support for the proposed assembly throughout February. Party spokesmen concentrated on criticising their opponents and the 40% rule, emphasising the essential modesty of the proposals in a positive way and arguing that the referendum had become a matter of self-confidence for the Scottish people. Analogies inevitably were made with the disastrous performance of the Scottish football team in the World Cup finals in Argentina the previous summer. The task now was to persuade voters to support what was on offer, as there was a real doubt that the 40% hurdle would be cleared by the 'yes' side. Writing in the *Glasgow Herald* towards the end of the month, Donald Stewart practically conceded that this was not going to happen when he stated that 'I am confident that Scotland will vote "yes" in the way that matters. That is that a majority of the electorate who take the trouble to vote will assert that Scots are capable of working together and making rational decisions'.[12]

These fears proved to be justified. While there was a small majority in favour of the government's proposals, the overall 'yes' vote was still some 7% short of the 40% barrier.[13] A more indecisive vote could not have been contrived. The government had already conceded that the 40% figure was not immutable as inaccuracies in the electoral register were bound to distort the result, and would therefore be taken into account when deciding whether to implement or not. Thus, it was not unlikely that the government would have proceeded with implementation on a 'yes' vote of 35 or 36%. As this figure was not quite reached, and there was a slim rather than a decisive majority in favour, Unionist critics of devolution were hardly going to be quiescent.

The S.N.P.'s National Council met two days after the referendum to consider what action should be taken, with reports in the press suggesting that the party would insist that the government now implement the Scotland Act.[14] An emergency resolution to this end was moved by Gordon Wilson and passed by acclamation by the 400 or so delegates. It declared that the S.N.P. was satisfied with the majority decision in the referendum, demanded 'that the government honour its manifesto commitment' to set up the assembly, and recommended S.N.P. M.P.s to 'seek an early general election' if this was not done.[15] What was most interesting about the meeting however, was the atmosphere of euphoria which apparently prevailed. The *Financial Times* reported that delegates 'were jubilant' and pressures were 'already building up to cut loose from the whole idea (of devolution) and go for a quick general election'.[16]

If nothing else, this was clear evidence of how unpopular the whole devolution adventure had become with those involved in the decision-making process. A few voices cautioned against a hasty attack on the government, but these were discounted. In an almost unprecedented action, a move was made to reject Margo McDonald's report to the National Council because it argued that a snap election which resulted in a Conservative victory would spell the end of any chance of an assembly and thus was not a good idea – a judgement which many have come to share in retrospect.[17] While the resolution which was approved did not specify exactly how long the M.P.s should sustain the government, William Wolfe was reported as saying that the parliamentary group would give the government 10–14 days, and other reports suggested no more than a month.[18]

As it turned out, George Reid's statement of 9 March that the government had 'less than two weeks' to put the Scotland Act into effect was most accurate, as the S.N.P. group decided on 23 March to vote against the government in a confidence motion.[19] If the S.N.P.'s primary intention was to see devolution through, then putting the government on notice was not a particularly realistic strategy for achieving it. The unpalatable truth was that the only option in this case was to play for time and hope to salvage something from the government's insecure position. While it could be argued that the threats over a timetable for implementation made by Mr Reid and later by Donald Stewart to the Prime Minister were negotiating counters rather than fixed demands, the group probably knew that the government would be unable to marshall sufficient support in this space of time in the light of the referendum result. Thus, the parliamentary group's tactics are better seen as responses to the internal pressures evident at Dundee rather than as actions designed to get the Scotland Act operational.

It came as no surprise, therefore, that after pressing the government for almost two weeks to have the Scotland Act voted on in the House, George Reid said on 19 March that the only way of now keeping it alive was to have a general election before this happened. By 23 March, the M.P.s had evidently concluded that the government could not force its dissident supporters into line, and that there was nothing to be gained by waiting for anything else to happen. It was time to deploy the ultimate weapon, despite the warnings and olive branches proffered simultaneously by the Prime Minister to the party. On 28 March, the S.N.P. parliamentary group voted with the opposition on a motion of no confidence, and the government was defeated by a single vote. Like all ultimate weapons, the S.N.P.'s sanction destroyed both the target and the sender, although this did not become fully apparent until after the election which was occasioned by the government's defeat in parliament.

Mullin (1979) remarks of the general election campaign that the party 'was so demoralised by its defeats that it hardly campaigned on a Scottish basis at all'.[20] While this presents a striking contrast to the apparent euphoria at Dundee after the referendum, and does not accord with the party chairman's own assessment of the probable level of S.N.P. support at an election to that meeting, it does reflect more objective realities. The Treasurer's report to the National Council (naturally lost in the post-referendum excitement), showed the branch dues to headquarters had fallen by 25% and income from the sale of membership cards had dropped 'by a staggering 40%' in the second half of 1978, an already bad year.[21] There was consequently a drastic reduction in central services and staff at a time when the party was in retreat within the electorate.

The best that could be hoped for was that the damage to the party's parliamentary representation would be minimised and that the campaign could be used to patch up some of the differences which had been created by devolution. The election campaign did indeed postpone a full post mortem on the devolution strategy for a further period. From the point of view of the incumbent leadership, this was a welcome breathing space in the light of the wave of hostile and atavistic sentiment evident at the March meeting of the National Council. A successful electoral performance might succeed in blunting some of the criticism, and in this sense, the S.N.P.'s election campaign was driven as much by internal as external necessities.

The election campaign, then, was something of an interregnum between the incipient revolution in March and its fruition at the annual party conference in September, in which the party office-holders used the advantages of incumbency to pursue policies which were not favoured by their rivals in the broader leadership, but which were electorally acceptable. Thus, the stampede to abandon devolution at the National Council was not translated into an electoral strategy of 'Independence – Nothing Less', and the campaign concentrated instead on the perfidious nature of the British parties and on a series of limited economic demands. The two major campaign leaflets launched successively and on 11 and 14 April bore the slogans, 'Broken promises – Labour style' and 'Broken promises – Tory style'.[22] Of the 44 press releases issued between 29 March and 2 May 1979, 21 were direct attacks on one or both of the major parties, a further seven dealt exclusively with devolution and six pointed to the tactical value of voting for the S.N.P. as a means of strengthening Scotland's bargaining position at Westminster.

The most striking aspect of the S.N.P.'s national campaign, however, was the absence of any direct mention of independence. Neither of the major statements of the party's constitutional position included the word. The supplementary manifesto said that the party did not stand for the break up of the U.K. 'as some of our opponents emotionally and wildly claim', but rather for the establishment of a 'new relationship under the crown . . . in an association of British states operating like the Nordic Union', and the other press statement on the subject talked of the need for 'our own parliament or assembly' in order to guarantee 'equality under the crown'.[23]

Whether these efforts to moderate the party's image made any difference to its performance is debatable in the context of the 'British' issues which dominated the election, and the S.N.P.'s low key campaigning. There certainly was a case for distancing the party from the government which was unpopular (although not particularly so in Scotland) for reasons unassociated with devolution. But a hard line separatist campaign was not likely to get anywhere when support was falling for devolution and rising for unionism (in the shape of the Conservative party). A return to separatism would only aggravate the party's decline.

At all events, the result of the general election was a disaster for the S.N.P. Its representation at Westminster was reduced from eleven to two, and its share of the Scottish vote sank from 30% to 17%. The Conservative victory ensured the removal of devolution from the policy arena for the forseeable future, and there was now nothing to restrain the forces of discontent which had been building up within the S.N.P. Had the party managed to retain a few more seats (and it was only narrowly beaten in a few instances), then the leadership's strategy of moderation may have paid off, so avoiding the plunge into atavism and recrimination which was to follow.

On balance then, the incumbent leadership behaved with a considerable degree of sensitivity towards public and party opinion alike in the circumstances of the referendum and election campaigns, as a national strategy of moderation was coupled with the concession of campaigning initiatives to local parties. This was a policy of damage limitation, in which the optimum outcome was the preservation of the party's parliamentary representation and the achievement of organisational stabilisation at the local level.

But as there was a fundamental discontinuity between the national campaigns and likely local initiatives, such an optimum outcome could not be expected. Either the national campaigns would succeed, in which case heavy organisational costs would be entailed, or local initiatives would predominate, in which case heavy electoral costs would be entailed. The fact that the party leaders had to adopt such a policy at all signified the increased salience of internal division in their calculations and the diminished nature of their authority. The behaviour of the parliamentary group in particular had never been more dominated by the imperatives of the party's internal politics.

Thus, by May 1979, the party had reached a stage in its development broadly in line with the model of third party growth suggested at the outset. The party leadership was no longer a coherent entity and its authority did not extend as far as it once had done. As we have already argued, the party's fortunes would have been better served if the leadership had behaved with more prudence in the three years leading up to the referendum.

The era of internal politics

The process of faction formation began almost immediately after the election, and was a direct consequence of the exposed position of the devolutionists in the incumbent leadership. While this was already apparent at the Dundee National Council, events at the June meeting suggested that the situation had deteriorated further. An acrimonious debate on staff redundancies led to a motion of no confidence in the chair (William Wolfe), and by implication in the leadership as a whole, being only narrowly defeated. This signalled a formal split in the party leadership between 'traditional-ists', and some of the leading pro-devolutionists, including Stephen Maxwell and Margo MacDonald. The latter had adjourned to a gathering of what was described as the 'S.N.P. socialist group' after the National Council was over. In publicly outlining the case for a social democratic strategy on 15 June, Stephen Maxwell brought this internal dispute into the open.[24]

The rival protagonists developed their arguments in submissions to the party's National Assembly, which had opened an official post-mortem on devolution. The traditionalists blamed the party's reversals on its flirtation with Westminster politics in general and with devolution in particular. The remedy entailed the complete abandonment of any support for devolution, the distancing of the party from Westminster and a return to the more proselytising style of a political movement. The social democrats and devolutionists on the other hand, criticised the party's lack of genuine commitment to devolution, and in particular its failure to mount an effective 'yes' campaign in the referendum.[25]

By the end of August, the process was complete. The 'revisionists' had consitituted themselves into the '79 Group' and were officially warned that they might be in breach of party rules. These developments were critical to the inversion of priorities which had been gradually taking place in the party. The formation of the '79 Group' was a recognition by the pro-devolutionary incumbents that they were now in a minority. They would have to defend their position through internal strategies rather than by producing electoral growth as had been the case in the 1970s. They were preparing for an orderly retreat in the face of the fundamentalist groundswell.

The reports by national office holders to the annual conference (which had been postponed until September), and resolutions to the conference have to be seen against the background of developing factionalism and the deep internal divisions created by the devolution strategy. Gordon Wilson's report said that the party would operate better if it was united, and the executive vice-chairman for organisation, noting that the party's referendum campaign had been 'erratic' because of internal opposition, concluded that the S.N.P. could no longer afford the luxury of each member choosing 'whether to accept or reject major democratic decisions of the party e.g. the referendum'.[26]

The formation of the '79 Group' did not prevent an initial blood-letting of the devolutionists among the incumbents. On the contrary; the tide of opinion at conference was running strongly in favour of the independence hardliners. Resolution 41, which had been sponsored by a record 21 branches and constituency associations, called upon delegates to reaffirm that independence was 'the aim of the S.N.P.', and to resolve 'that independence will be the principal theme on which the party and all its candidates will campaign in all future parliamentary general and by-elections'.[27] An amendment from Edinburgh North constituency supporting devolution as an interim measure was defeated, while one from Pennywell/Muirhouse branch resolving that the party would 'not engage in any more dealings in assemblies, devolution or meaningful talks' was carried as part of the amended main resolution.[28]

This policy shift was accompanied by the removal of those most closely identified with devolution from the most senior positions in the party. The elections for national office bearers saw the replacement of pro-devolutionists such as Margo MacDonald, Stephen Maxwell and William Wolfe by independence hardliners such as Douglas Henderson (elected as senior vice-chairman), Robert McIntyre (elected as party president), Jim Fairlie (elected as executive vice-chairman for policy) and Gordon Wilson (elected as party chairman). According to one report, this fundamentalist coup was supported by those traditional nationalists who had been eclipsed since the pragmatist take-over in the early 1970s. It was now the latter's turn to lose office. Thus, the readiness of conference to put the blame for the party's current difficulties on the shoulders of those who had advocated devolution was not without its benefits for some.

However, the reversion to fundamentalism and the turnover in the leadership at conference did not end the crisis within the party. On the contrary, it was only the beginning. The conference decisions were essentially provisional in nature, and signified that one era in the party's history was over rather than that a new one had begun. Such major changes in the organisational status quo were symptomatic of the general process of destabilisation and decline which had been underway for some time, but which only now assumed its full proportions. By August 1979, the party's standing in the polls was down to 12%, and by the end of the year party H.Q. had a revenue deficit of £20,000, having raised only £500 in the financial appeal to delegates attending the annual conference.[29]

The displaced leaders had regrouped for a rearguard action under the auspices of the '79 Group'. Thus, while the main policies and personalities of the Group were decisively defeated at conference, this did not result in the Group disbanding itself. It had every reason not to. It had a definite power base within the more broadly defined leadership of the party (i.e. the National Council and the elected members of the N.E.C.), and in the localities among those who had supported the devolutionary road. Second, in committing the N.E.C. to organise 'direct action' against the dumping of nuclear waste in Scotland, conference had given the '79 Group' a new issue to involve itself with. Third, it had also been decided to breathe life into a legacy of the pre-referendum period, namely the industrial strategy.[30]

The firm basis for factional conflict was to result in frequent alterations in policy and changes in leadership, and continuing electoral and organisational shrinkage over the following few years. During this period, the debate over the party's orientation revolved around four main campaigns – the industrial strategy, the new oil campaign (1980), the Scottish Resistance campaign

(1981) and the Scottish Alternative campaign (1982) – none of which should really have taken place at all if the 'Independence – Nothing Else' policy of 1979 was seriously intended. The progress of these campaigns proved in practice to be little more than a barometer of the balance of power prevailing within the party at the time, and bore little relation to the state of public opinion. If a policy review process was taking place, then it was a particularly destructive one which brought the party to its lowest ebb for more than fifteen years.

The industrial campaign typified the ambiguities in the party at this time. An inheritance from the old order, it was retained after a change in personnel. The industrial liaison officer (a founder member of the '79 Group'), had been made redundant in the organisational cuts imposed in June, and overall responsibility passed from Tom McAlphine to the incoming executive vice-chairman for policy (Jim Fairlie) after the 1979 conference. Aimed to increase S.N.P. influence in the trade unions and among Labour voters, the capaign was strongly 'leftist' and syndicalist in orientation, and from the outset involved various forms of 'direct action'. Thus, the activists took part in various campaigns against factory closures and redundancies, and attempted (unsuccessfully) to spread party organisation directly into the trade unions and workplaces.

While no longer tinged with a devolutionary hue (owing to Mr Fairlie's influence), this strategy was the natural terrain of those who had joined the '79 Group', for it required the continuance of the leftward drift which had been advocated since the mid 1970s by the displaced leaders. It would also devolve campaigning initiative back to the localities and weaken the position of the national leadership. On the other hand, it was both tactically and strategically alien to the ascendant traditionalists, who were hostile to the importation of 'class' issues, and who were not used to joining factory occupations and the like. Not surprisingly then, the industrial strategy (and its 'Scottish Resistance' successor), found little support among the newly installed office holders.[31]

In opposition to the 'direct action' strategies promoted by the '79 Group' and its sympathisers, was the new oil campaign and later, the 'Scottish Alternative' campaign. Evidently inspired by the new party chairman Gordon Wilson, the oil campaign was a centrist and centralist antidote to the industrial strategy. The new campaign followed on from a lengthy resolution sponsored by the National Council at the 1980 annual conference held in May.[32] Using the tested formula of the 1972 campaign, the 1980 campaign set itself exactly the same objectives, viz: to show the value of the oil, show how it could be used to provide employment opportunities and show how the U.K. government was benefiting from it at Scotland's expense.[33] This time, it was accorded a very different reaction from within the party however.

Before the initiative was even launched, it was reported that the '79 Group' was planning an unemployment campaign which would directly clash with the oil campaign, for the real significance of the latter lay in its role as a leadership counter-strategy to the '79 Group'. This became apparent when the party's National Council met in December 1980. In tandem with a move by the N.E.C. to have all internal groups banned, Gordon Wilson launched a three pronged attack on the Group, using the oil issue as one of his weapons. He said that the oil issue 'should never have been dropped as it largely was in 1975',[34] a barbed reference to the mothballing of the original campaign by those who were now leading members of the '79 Group'. Second, in contradiction to the '79 Group' strategy of pushing the S.N.P. to the left, he argued that the S.N.P. would only win Labour seats if it could also attract Conservative voters; finally he said that the ill-effects of factionalism on the Labour Party should be a lesson to the S.N.P. However, the resolution outlawing official groups, which had originally been aimed at a right-wing splinter group (Siol nan Gaidhael), was defeated when it became clear that the '79 Group' was a principal target.

Thus, final victory for the counter-revolution begun in 1979 was not achieved on this occasion. Mr Wilson nevertheless continued to press his case. In his report to the March 1981 meeting of the National Council, he drew attention to the substantial block of support for the newly formed Social Democratic Party (S.D.P.) in Scotland, and warned against the S.N.P. moving too far to the left. However, the hope that the oil campaign would prevent this faded when what had been described as 'the hottest political issue of the eighties'[35] turned out to be a completely damp squib. Had the campaign been successful, then Mr Wilson might have consolidated the hold of the 'new' leaders on the party in early 1981 without the need for a purge of the '79 Group', and certainly without the debacle of the party's attempts at civil disobedience associated with the 'Scottish Resistance' campaign.

It was in the context of the failures of the oil campaign and the industrial strategy that the burgeoning of the 'Scottish Resistance' campaign and the '79 Group' was possible. In the lead-in to the 1981 conference, William Wolfe was quoted as saying that there was now massive support in the S.N.P. for direct action, and reports in the press suggested that incumbents such as Gordon

Wilson had already resigned themselves to accepting it.[36] The idea was not new, and had grown out of the limited involvement in the industrial and anti-nuclear campaigns approved by the 1979 and 1980 conferences, supported by the '79 Group' but not acted upon by the party leadership for reasons we have already suggested.[37] The strategy was formalised in resolution 3 to the 1981 annual conference which was sponsored by two of the most left wing party locals (Glasgow Govan constituency association and Uddingston/Bothwell branch). It not only advocated 'direct action up to and including political strikes and civil disobedience on a mass scale', but it insisted that the N.E.C. organise a campaign 'as a matter of urgency'. A crippling amendment to the resolution was defeated, and it was carried without significant alteration.

This policy coup was again accompanied by significant changes in the party hierarchy. In the election for executive vice-chairman for policy, Gordon Murray was defeated by Jim Sillars, and Andrew Currie was elected as executive vice-chairman for organis-ation. Both of them were prominent supporters of the '79 Group'. Furthermore, Group members took half the vacant seats on the N.E.C. elected by National Council in June. The immediate fruit of this change in the balance of power was a renewed attempt to increase S.N.P. influence in the labour movement. Support was given to a factory occupation picket, and was accompanied by a somewhat disastrous participation in a demonstration in favour of the workforce which had been made redundant. Government Job Centres across Scotland were also occupied by party members.

However, the authority of conference decisions proved once more to be less than total and the revolution was short-lived. When a policy did emerge from the N.E.C., it looked very different from the radical proposals of resolution 3. The National Council meeting in September was informed by the chairman (Gordon Wilson), that the N.E.C. had decided to adopt an integrated campaigning strategy in which the Scottish Resistance 'theme' would give way in late September to 'a political and economic campaign' designed to build credibility and recruit members. This would essentially follow the format of an election campaign. Noting that conference decisions on civil disobedience had 'upset a few of our members', Mr Wilson said that it was a 'a minor area of activity compared with our need to rebuild the party organisation-ally . . . (and) to regain mass electoral support'. The report concluded that 'what may appeal to us as S.N.P. activists will not go down with voters we are required to gain'.[38]

The N.E.C.'s proposal hardly reflected the wishes of conference, let alone those most in favour of direct action. Notwithstanding the perfunctory reference to the 'Scottish Resistance', this was nothing less than a dismissal of the civil disobedience strategy. If further confirmation of this were needed, it was reported at the end of the month that party headquarters was resisting deployment of the 'Scottish Resistance' theme.[39] Given the short projected duration of the campaign, any delay would minimise its impact.

The symbolic occupation of the Royal High School building in Edinburgh on 16 October by Jim Sillars and five others (as least three of whom, including Sillars were members of the '79 Group'), has to be seen in this context. It was as much a protest against the maneouvrings of the incumbent leadership of the S.N.P. as it was against the absence of a Scottish Assembly in the building.[40] There was a predictably hostile response within the executive, with three of its members dissociating themselves publicly from the action and, along with Donald Stewart, refusing to attend the support rally for the occupation on 24 October.[41] Mr Sillars argued at the December meeting of the National Council that he had only been carrying out party policy anyway, and was therefore 'entitled to the public silence of senior office holders'.[42] This was hardly an unreasonable view in the context of the conference 'mandate' for a massive campaign of civil disobedience.

As press reports had already suggested however, while the conference may have been a triumph for the '79 Group', the traditionalists never accepted defeat. Thus, there was a renewed assault on the '79 Group' at the December meeting of the National Council. The chairman's report described the 'Scottish Resistance' campaign as 'negative', argued that the party should instead put forward 'a constructive, attractive and creative programme' and reiterated the view that it was simply not possible to win a large number of seats unless the party could take the 'moderate vote'.[43] The National Secretary effectively terminated the 'Scottish Resistance' by announcing that the 'Scottish Alternative' campaign, described as an S.N.P. version of the 'New Deal', would be launched on 23 January, and although a resolution to proscribe the '79 Group' from 1 January was defeated, an N.E.C. resolution instructing the '79 Group' to obey the party constitution was approved by 235 votes to 67.[44]

This decision proved to the first step on the road to the ultimate dissolution of the Group, and the expulsions which followed. In the period between the December meeting and the annual conference in May, there were still instances of 'direct action' taking place, primarily in the industrial field, and it was perhaps these which finally galvanised the 'traditionalists' into taking some direct action of their own. This consisted in forming a rival group (the Campaign for Nationalism in Scotland), and then supporting a move by Gordon Wilson to outlaw all factions at the conference. Once this was approved, the Campaign would voluntarily dissolve itself with the implications that all other groups would do the same.

The first day of the conference proved decisive for this strategy: encouraged by the failure of the '79 Group' to secure a reaffirmation of the civil disobedience policy on the first day, Mr Wilson threatened to resign if conference did not support him. Arguing that the Group was part of 'a disease that has affected the party for some time',[45] Mr Wilson at least chose an opportune moment for his action. The news media were dominated by the Falklands conflict and the papal visit to Scotland. Thus, the S.N.P.'s troubles were not likely to figure as prominently as they would do in normal circumstances. The party's 'gravest crisis' was resolved in favour of Mr Wilson by a vote of 308 to 188, and all factions were given three months to dissolve themselves or face expulsion if they did not.

This almost precipitated the withdrawal of the S.N.P.'s candidate and '79 Group' member, Ron Wylie, from the Coatbridge and Airdrie by-election which was in progress at the time, as Group members sought ways to preserve the Group's right to exist. While the threat was made, the option was not pursued. The '79 Group' did, however, try to preclude Mr Wilson from standing for the chairmanship of the party, a move which the conference also rejected.

This overall process produced all the usual symptoms with which the party had now become familiar. There was a significant turnover within the leadership, and while Stephen Maxwell was the only prominent '79 Group' casualty at conference elections for national officers, the rout of the left was confirmed when leading '79 Group' members failed to get elected onto the party's N.E.C. at the June meeting of the National Council. The Treasurer's annual financial report showed that the party's financial position had slipped from surplus to deficit over the previous year, representing a tunaround of some £20,000. The decline in membership was reflected in a much reduced sale of membership cards to branches and a shortfall in dues from branches to party H.Q.[46]

The expulsion of seven former members of the '79 Group' for breaching party rules duly took place in November after they had tried to set up a new organisation following the voluntary dissolution of the '79 Group' in September. The demise of the Group therefore began only six months after its greatest triumphs, and although it took a further ten months or so to secure its final liquidation, Mr Wilson's report to the December meeting of the National Council signalled the completion of this operation. In observing that a 'civil war has been raging since 1979' in the party, Mr Wilson acknowledged the dominance of internal politics in that period; the party had 'become overconcerned with fringe issues to the exclusion of our main goal of national freedom'. The task now was to reconstruct the party before the next election.[47]

While the number of eventual expulsions was small, and most of the prominent former '79-ers' now occupy leading positions in the S.N.P. the immediate effect was entirely negative. Many local sympathisers of the Group left the party by resigning or simply not renewing their membership, and in many instances subsequently joined the Labour Party. This was something of a hollow victory then. After three years of internal conflict and useless campaigning, the party had touched its lowest ebb for a generation. It had lost many of its most active members, and was now in the hands of what appeared to some to be a semi-gerontocracy. On the other hand, it was also a necessary victory for those now in control: in finally clearing out the influence of the pragmatists who had controlled the party leadership in the 1970s, the process had brought others to prominence and their positions were secure, at least for the time being.

The overall balance sheet 1979–82

It is clear that the S.N.P. was already a divided party by 1979 and that the level of internal conflict was rising. While the incumbent leadership which had run the party during the 1970s was still in control of the national campaigning effort in the referendum and general election, this has to be set in the context of its weakened authority in the localities, its internal division and its diminished logistical capabilities resulting from organisational decline. A serious shrinkage of the party's electoral and membership bases had already take place by 1979, and these depredations coalesced as visibly adverse influences on the S.N.P.'s campaigning capacities.

Using the advantages of incumbency, the leadership pursued a strategy of damage limitation in these two campaigns. The effect was to postpone rather than to prevent the purge which had been intimated in March, and the 'factionalisation' of the leadership thus followed immediately after the election was over. From this point onward, an internal civil war raged in the broadly defined party leadership until 1982. During this period, there was a battle for power and control between resurgent 'traditionalists' and displaced 'pragmatists' in which neither faction secured a decisive victory until the expulsion of the '79 Group' in 1982.

Election to or displacement from key party posts did not prove to be a conclusive factor in this battle for two reasons. First, there was no consolidation of power because of an almost annual turnover of incumbents and challengers in these posts and in the overall balance of the N.E.C., and second, the 'winners' had to contend with, and the 'losers' could take advantage of, the multi-office power base which party rules and procedures facilitated. Losing an election for office bearer would still not preclude membership of the N.E.C. via selection from the National Council, and representation on the National Council was more or less guaranteed either through election at annual conference or nomination from a local association. In addition to these forums was the National Assembly, the various N.E.C. sub-committees and formal or informal 'groups' themselves before this form of faction was outlawed. Thus, as predicted, the relatively open and competitive structure of the party leadership proved to be conducive to factional activity. On the other hand, the inconclusive nature of conference decisions and the lack of involvement of the general membership in the various policy 'initiatives' suggest that the roots of factionalism were not to be found at this lower level.

The failure to improve the party's electoral performance was contributory to factional activity, which in turn inhibited the development of any effective electoral strategies. Thus, massive losses were sustained at the local elections in 1980, and there was an overall regression in performance by 1982 to the 1970 level. While these losses cannot be entirely attributed to the party's internal difficulties, the latter made nothing but a negative contribution to the party's standing. There had been an overall inversion of priorities with internal politics dominating over electoral politics, and until the subordination of campaigning initiatives to internal competition was ended the electoral situation was unlikely to improve. Although this had been developing gradually as competition within the leadership intensified from 1976, the fissure of 1979 marked a turning point. The organisational consequence of this process was a continual reduction in party membership and the income from it, so that by the end of the period, party membership was down to the 1965 level.

Notes

[1] J. Bochel and D. Denver, 'Local Campaigning', in Bochel *et al.*, *The Referendum Experience*, p. 43, Table 3.1.

[2] Macartney, 'The Protagonists', in Bochel *et al.*, p. 18.

[3] Macartney argues that this was 'consonant with the party's decentralist ethos', Macartney, 'The Protagonists', in Boichet *et al.*, p. 18. See also Bochel and Denver, 'Local Campaigning' in Bochel *et al.*, p. 45, and M. Dyer, 'Aberdeen and the Grampian Region', in Bochel *et al.*, p. 62.

[4] Macartney, 'The Protagonists', in Bochel *et al.*, p. 38, Table 2.13a.

[5] Bochel and Denver, 'Local Campaigning', in Bochel *et al.*, p. 52. Macartney's figures for central expenditure show that the S.N.P.'s central spending was lower than that of either the Liberal Party or the Communist Party of Great Britain. Macartney, 'The Protagonists', in Bochel *et al.*, p. 31, T. 2.8.

[6] Report by the executive vice-chairman for organisation to the National Council, Scottish National Party, Edinburgh, 3 March 1979. See report in *The Scotsman*, 28 February 1979; Dyer, 'Aberdeen and the Grampian Region' in Bochel *et al.*, p. 63, and C. Mullin, 'Edinburgh's Silence', in Bochel *et al.*, p. 89.

[7] R. Perman, 'The Devolution Referendum Campaign of 1979', in H. M. Drucker and N. L. Drucker (eds.), *The Scottish Government Yearbook 1980*, Edinburgh, Paul Harris, 1980, p. 54.

[8] See previous chapter and Miller, *The End of British Politics?*, p. 248. It was clearly the intention of the devolutionists in the party leadership that party locals should co-operate with other parties. Thus, the *Glasgow Herald* reported Stephen Maxwell (a senior member of the S.N.P.'s executive), as saying that party branches and associations 'are being encouraged to find scope for co-operation with other parties', see report in the *Glasgow Herald*, 23 January 1979. However, as the referendum study by Bochel *et al.* suggests, co-operation was only patchy. See Bochel *et al.*, *The Referendum Experience*, chs. 3 and 4.

[9] Macartney, 'The Protagonists', in Bochel *et al.*, p. 38, T. 2.13a.

[10] See press, release 10 January 1979, Scottish National Party, Edinburgh, and report in *The Guardian*, 12 January 1979.

[11] See report in the *Glasgow Herald*, 25 January 1979.

[12] See report in the *Glasgow Herald*, 23 February 1979.

[13] The final results were: 'Yes' 1,230,937 (33%); 'No' 1,153,502 (31%); 'yes' majority 77,435. See report in *The Scotsman*, 3 March 1979.

[14] See reports in the *Financial Times*, and *The Guardian*, 3 March 1979.

[15] Minutes of the National Council ref. NC 79/1, Scottish National Party, Edinburgh, 3 March 1979.

[16] The *Financial Times*, 5 March 1979.

[17] Minutes of the National Council ref. NC 79/5, Scottish National Party, Edinburgh, 3 March 1979.

[18] See reports in *The Observer*, 4 March 1979, the *Financial Times*, 5 March 1979, and *The Scotsman*, 6 March 1979. However, two of those who had attended the Dundee National Council and who were interviewed in 1982, said that the time limit was 90 days.

[19] See press release, 9 March 1979, Scottish National Party, Edinburgh.

[20] Mullin, 'The Scottish National Party', in Drucker (ed.), *Multi-Party Britain*, p. 130.

[21] Report by the Treasurer to the National Council, Scottish National Party, Edinburgh, 3 March 1979.

[22] See press releases, 11 and 14 April 1979, Scottish National Party, Edinburgh.

[23] Supplementary Manifesto, Scottish National Party, Edinburgh, 11 April 1979, and press release, 1 May 1979, Scottish National Party, Edinburgh.

[24] See report in *The Scotsman*, 15 June 1979.

[25] See submissions by P. McLennan, Ross and Cromarty constituency association, 10 August 1979, A. Carmichael, Glasgow Cathcart constituency association, 9 August 1979, and W. McRae, 19 August 1979, Scottish National Party, Edinburgh, 1979. See submissions by S. Maxwell, 9 August 1979, I. Lindsay, 10 August 1979, T. Wilson, 9 August 1979, A. McAlindin, 9 August 1979, Scottish National Party, Edinburgh, 1979.

[26] Reports to the 45th annual conference by the executive vice-chairman for organisation and from Gordon Wilson (on behalf of the parliamentary group), Scottish National Party, Edinburgh, 1979.

[27] Agenda to the 45th annual conference, resolution 41, 15 September 1979, Scottish National Party, Edinburgh, 1979.

[28] Outcome of business on conference agenda, Scottish National Party, Edinburgh, September 1979. See reports in *The Guardian* and the *Financial Times* 17 September 1979.

[29] The S.N.P.'s standing in the polls was down to 12% according to the *Glasgow Herald*'s 'System Three' survey in August (see report in the *Glasgow Herald*, 15 August 1979) and by the end of the year, the party had a revenue deficit of over £20,000. The financial appeal at conference had raised £500 only; Report by the Treasurer to the National Council, Scottish National Party, Edinburgh, 1 November 1979.

[30] On 'direct action', see agenda to the 45th annual conference, resolutions 1 and 10 especially, 13 September 1979, Scottish National Party, Edinburgh, 1979.

[31] With the exception of Mr Fairlie, none of those who could be considered as 'traditionalists' on the independence question participated in these initiatives.

[32] Agenda to the 46th annual conference, resolution 8, 29 May 1980, Scottish National Party, Edinburgh, 1980.

[33] See press release, 25 September 1980, Scottish National Party, Edinburgh. As in 1972, support material was prepared for party members to use.

[34] Chairman's report to the National Council, Scottish National Party, Edinburgh, 6 December 1980.

[35] See press release, 25 September 1980, Scottish National Party, Edinburgh.

[36] See report in *Sunday Standard*, 24 May 1981.

[37] William Wolfe hinted that the leadership had been dragging its feet on 'direct action' in early May; see report in *The Scotsman*, 6 May 1981. See Agenda to the 47th annual conference, resolution 3, 28 May 1981, Scottish National Party, Edinburgh, 1981, and see report in the *Glasgow Herald*, 28 May 1981.

[38] Chairman's report to the National Council, Scottish National Party, Edinburgh, 5 September 1981.

[39] See reports in the *Glasgow Herald*, 25 September and 2 October 1981.

[40] The decision to occupy the building which would have housed the Scottish Assembly provided for in the Scotland Act, was announced after the September meeting of the National Council. See report in *The Scotsman*, 10 September 1981.

[41] The executive members were Jim Fairlie, Margaret Bain and Winnie Ewing. Ron Wylie, a leading member of the 79 Group criticised them for refusing to attend the Calton Hill rally. See report in the *Glasgow Herald*, 20 September 1981.

[42] Report by the executive vice-chairman for policy to the National Council, Scottish National Party, Edinburgh, 5 December 1981.

[43] Chairman's report to the National Council, Scottish National Party, Edinburgh, 5 December 1981.

[44] Minutes of the National Council ref. NC 81/61, Scottish National Party, Edinburgh, 5 December 1981.

[45] The resolution outlawing groups was approved of by 308–188. See report in the *Glasgow Herald*, 7 June 1982.

[46] Agenda to the 48th annual conference, resolution 14, 3 June 1982, Scottish National Party, Edinburgh, 1982. On elections from the National Council to the N.E.C. and party finances, see report in the *Glasgow Herald*, 21 June 1982.

[47] Chairman's report to the National Council, Scottish National Party, Edinburgh, 4 December 1982. On expulsions, see reports in the *Glasgow Herald*, 28 June and 12 November 1982, *The Scotsman*, 1 September and 1 November 1982.

CHAPTER 6

The New Separatist Coalition

In common with much else, Scottish politics have been radically affected by ten years of Thatcherism. While the results of this aspect of the Thatcher revolution have been a long time in coming, they are none the less profound for that. Since 1979, a new separatist coalition has been in the making in Scotland. Comprised of the S.N.P., the Labour Party, and assorted pressure groups ranging in size from the Scottish Trades Union Congress S.T.U.C. to the Campaign for a Scottish Assembly (C.S.A.), it now represents a powerful consensus among the opinion-forming classes in Scotland. There are disagreements on the specifics, but the coalition is defined by its unambiguously nationalist orientation on the constitutional issue and its socialistic ideology.

It is evident from the foregoing chapters that such a coalition might never have emerged if it had been left simply to the Nationalists to create it. Indeed, as the nationalist revival has gathered pace, the principal partners in the coalition have been increasingly at each others' throats. As Labour and the S.N.P. compete for advantage on the same issues for the same voters, relations between them both inside and outside parliament have started to deteriorate. As in the case of the former Alliance partners, closeness of policy has not guaranteed harmony – on the contrary, it has only intensified competition between them.

The S.N.P. has never enjoyed particularly good relationships with the Labour Party, however, and with the politics of faction dominating party affairs in the late 1970s and early 1980s, the Nationalists were in no position to initiate coalitions with other parties. While undoubtedly benefiting from the creation of the coalition, the S.N.P. has played an intermittent rather than a dominant role in its development. In contrast to the 1970s, it is the Labour Party itself which has been making much of the

110

running, unwittingly pushing the self-destruct buttons in the process.

How has this happened? From the vantage points of the 1960s and 1970s, it would have been absurd to argue that the Labour Party either promoted or supported nationalism in Scotland. For reasons that had more to do with electoral expediency than a moral or philosophical commitment to Home Rule, the Wilson government established the Royal Commission on the Constitution in 1969, and subsequently forced a devolution package on a reluctant Scottish Labour leadership in 1974. There seems little reason to disagree with Tam Dalyell's verdict on the 1978 Scotland Act that 'the whole devolution caper . . . has been . . . primarily an exercise in party politics. . . The legislation was hastily cobbled together to meet the electoral threat posed by the Scottish National Party'.[1] During the great devolution 'debate' in the 1970s, doubts about Labour's real commitment to devolution were never far from the surface.

Since the defeat of the Labour government in 1979, however, the Labour Party has moved towards a much clearer commitment to Scottish Home Rule with the party in Scotland taking up an increasingly nationalist position on this issue. In short, it has been Tartanised. Egged on by a nationalist lobby in the S.T.U.C., the Co-operative Party and all-party groups such as the C.S.A., the Scottish party has pushed radical devolution proposals through the Labour Party nationally. The party in Scotland has evidently convinced itself that a Scottish Assembly would have protected Scotland from the worst depredations of the 'Thatcher revolution'.

Until 1988, the magnitude of this process was not evident electorally, even if there were already signs of an organisational upswing in the S.N.P.[2] However, Jim Sillars's victory for the S.N.P. at the Glasgow Govan by-election in November 1988 has exposed the full proportions of Labour's vulnerability. As the inheritor of the S.N.P.'s devolutionary nationalism of the 1970s, Labour has done much to prepare the ground for a nationalist revival. Like Dr Frankenstein, Labour politicians in Scotland have created a monster which threatens to run completely out of control. A crushing defeat for Labour in one of its safest seats in Britain was bad enough. That it also revealed deep divisions in Labour's ranks on the national question and a continuing organisational malaise induced by the selection procedures made it an incomparably worse proposition. It is not surprising therefore, that complacency has been replaced by confusion. While some of those most culpable for the nationalist revival have been back-peddling furiously, others have further embraced the nationalist cause. This tendency, now epitomised by the Scottish Labour Action (S.L.A.) group, continues to increase its influence steadily within the party in Scotland.

This development has been fortuitous for the S.N.P., as its movement away from fundamentalism and towards a more pragmatic, left-leaning nationalism has been a hesitant process. In contrast to the position in the mid 1970s, the party now is neither as pragmatic in its nationalism nor as moderate in its 'leftness' as it was then. This has been well-illustrated by the party's decision effectively to withdraw from the all-party constitutional convention established in February 1989 on the one hand, and its militant opposition to the government's community charge on the other. To some extent, the S.N.P.'s 'stiffness' shows that it still bears the scars of the lengthy period of factionalism ushered in after the referendum and general election of 1979. The commitment to 'socialist-nationalism' inherent in the current strategy of attacking the Labour vote has proved a bitter pill for some 'traditionalist' party members to swallow, and it may ultimately destabilise the party's traditionally heterogeneous support base outside of the major cities. There is still a good deal of life left in S.N.P. fundamentalism, and as on previous occasions, obituaries have been somewhat premature in writing it off.

Whatever its consequences however, current policy represents a striking transformation in contrast to the fundamentalist counter-revolution which reached its apogee in 1982. The S.N.P. remains divided on ideological grounds, but the balance has now tipped firmly towards the pragmatic left. Fortunately for the Nationalists, the intensity of the divide has been obscured, and even moderated, by the spectacle of Labour's unfolding nationalism. Until the establishment of the Constitutional Convention, the pragmatists were able to take up harder constitutional positions, and thus offend traditional nationalists less, because of this development. Irrespective of the S.N.P.'s decision to boycott the Convention, the split between constitutional fundamentalists and pragmatists might well be greater were it not for Labour's current policies. As we will argue, the Nationalists have already made a major impact on the Convention through its founding document, and it is the S.N.P. rather than Labour which may ultimately gain most from it.

Thus, this chapter cannot be simply about the S.N.P. In order to document the coalesence of the policies of the the principal partners in the coalition, we shall first examine the reconstruction of the S.N.P. since 1982, and then analyse the key elements in the transformation of the Labour Party in Scotland. Finally, we shall offer some explanations of the coalition based on different assumptions about the nature of parties and voters in Scotland.

The Reconstruction of the S.N.P.

In the wake of the 1988 Govan by-election, support for the S.N.P. rose to levels not seen since the mid 1970s, and support for independence reached unprecedented heights according to some opinion surveys.[3] Despite some post-Govan slippage, the revival long predicted by the Nationalists themselves is apparently underway, with the party receiving its second best ever national result (25·6% of the votes cast), at the elections for the European Parliament in June 1989.

As recently as the June 1987 general election, the S.N.P. achieved only 14% of the Scottish vote, a result which itself compared favourably with the party's performance over the previous few years. At the height of the fundamentalist counter-revolution in 1982–83, the party polled 10% of the vote at the 1982 Regional Council elections, and under 12% of the Scottish vote at the 1983 general election. In 1983, support for independence among S.N.P. voters stood at only 34%, devolution was identified as the most significant political issue by less than 0·05% of Scottish voters and independence was supported by only 13% of all Scottish voters.[4] If the process of electoral reconstruction had continued at the same pace as 1983–87, then it would have taken decades rather than months for the S.N.P. to reach 30% in the opinion polls.

The electoral transformation of the S.N.P. since 1987 is thus remarkable. If the Govan campaign was a devastating indictment of Labour's organisational and political weaknesses, then it equally symbolised the S.N.P.'s rebirth. The Sillars campaign showed the S.N.P. organisationally revitalised and politically transformed compared to the period of 'civil war' experienced in the early 1980s. The key elements of the campaign – the assault on the Labour vote through an 'opening to the left', the apparently new constitutional 'option' of independence within the European Community, and the renewed effort at 'doorstep' campaigning and effective canvassing – in fact represented the accumulated fruits of five years of change. While the importance of the S.N.P.'s own contributions to its revival should not be overstated, they were undoubtedly significant in the particular circumstances of Govan and, so it is proving, Scottish politics post-Govan.

In contrast to earlier nationalist surges, the organisational revival of the party has been steady rather than spectacular, although it has followed the same broad pattern. The decline in party membership halted around 1983, since when increasing numbers of new younger members have been recruited. This has in turn provided an increased level of funding available for campaign purposes, enabling the party, for example, to send the national organiser to the United States to study presidential campaigning techniques, and to conduct an exhaustive canvas and post-election study of voting patterns at Govan.

In structural terms, however, the S.N.P. has changed very little, retaining the same basic organisational format of the 1960s and 1970s. Membership growth has thus been achieved within the same framework of national and local participation which characterised the previous growth cycle. The enduring reliance on the party membership as a campaigning resource has precluded any further centralisation, despite proposals to the contrary. Subsequent to the '79 Group' fiasco, a Commission of Inquiry into party organisation was established by Gordon Wilson in 1983. Announcing the findings of the Commission in February 1985, the National Secretary, Neil MacCallum, said that the party had become 'too bureaucratic, too introspective and too conservative'.[5] In what amounted to the biggest reorganisation for twenty years, it was proposed that the National Assembly be scrapped and the central leadership be strengthened by the appointment of a general convenor and a general secretary, and the streamlining of the N.E.C. All these recommendations were rejected by the special conference convened to consider them, along with the attempt to constitutionalise group activity in an effort to build links with trade unions, to Campaign for Nuclear Disarmament and presumably the C.S.A.

Within this organisational framework, there has been a decisive shift in the centre of political gravity accompanied by a slow (if unpredictable) decline in the intensity of factional politics. The growing strength of the pragmatic left within the party, and the heavy Labour majorities in Scotland at the 1983 and 1987 elections, has made possible a sustained 'opening to the left'. Essentially, this has consisted of targeting the Labour vote on a number of specific social and economic issues (such as opposition to the community charge), and gradually adopting a more conciliatory position on all-party proposals for constitutional change. From outright hostility to the C.S.A. and a Constitutional Convention, the S.N.P. has officially moved towards support and participation, albeit on its own (as yet unsatisfied) terms. On non-constitutional issues, a number of tactics have been resurrected from the 'civil war' era (the industrial campaigns), while others (such as the commitment to a 'Workers' Charter' and the community charge non-payment campaign), are new. Since Labour's policy review, the Nationalists are also pressing Labour hard on unilateralism, and have even sought to act as the custodian of trade union militancy during the dispute between the local government workers and their employers in 1989.

The extent of the transformation can be gauged by comparing the present orientation of the party with that in 1983. In 1983, the party was suffering the effects of the period of factional activity which had culminated in the expulsion of seven prominent '79 Group' members in 1982. This was causing continued internal disruption and a consequent delay in the normal processes of the party. Thus, despite attempts to rescind the expulsions, the act of contrition demanded by the N.E.C. provoked resignations among former Group members in the localities, and when a general election was announced in May 1983, S.N.P. candidate selections were still to be made in over a third of the 72 Scottish constituencies.

As for policy, the fundamentalist stranglehold on the party's decision-making forums meant that the S.N.P. gave no specific support to devolution during the election campaign. However, there was a dichotomy between party activists and office-seeking leaders on the convention issue. Both Gordon Wilson and Jim Sillars promoted the idea (which the party has latterly supported), of a Scottish convention of all 'pro-assembly' Scottish M.P.s and pressure groups in the eventuality of another Conservative victory. Aiming specifically at the Labour vote, the party was projected as a pressure group which would 'protect Scotland against the next five years of Thatcherism'. Mr Sillars claimed that many Scottish Labour M.P.s supported the idea of an 'emergency' convention, and invited the S.T.U.C. to participate on the grounds that 'there is no group in Scotland with a greater interest in a Scottish Parliament than the trade union movement'.[6]

As it turned out, there was no majority for this position when the party's annual conference convened at Rothesay in September. The fundamentalists opposed a convention on the grounds that it would have no 'mandate' from the sovereign Scottish people, and conference rejected participation in a such a body. Despite as subsequent reversal of this position, to which pro-convention party members now refer to justify their own participation, this decision has arguably proved to be the more lasting. The only concession made to moderation on the constitutional question was contained in resolution 22 which, in affirming the goal of independence, stated that the party was not 'seeking to obstruct the advent of any step or steps which could return to Scotland limited legislative and economic powers'. As Gordon Wilson said, this represented a change of image rather than a change in the substance of the policy of 'independence – nothing less'.

The failure by the party leadership to get retrospective endorsement for its campaigning in the election made little difference to its subsequent behaviour. As on previous occasions, the decisions of the annual conference were simply ignored. Thus, the period after 1983 saw the gradual ebb of the fundamentalist tide rather than its continued flow. Having apparently received a rap on the knuckles from the fundamentalists, the newly elected party leadership in alliance with a reviving gradualist left, continued to express heretical sentiments. In advance of the 1984 annual conference held in Inverness, Jim Fairlie, the senior vice-chairman and independence hardliner, resigned his position in protest at the number of pro-devolutionists on the N.E.C., and announced that he would oppose the resolutions calling for affiliation to the C.S.A. and the establishment of an elected Scottish Convention. In a confidential report to the N.E.C., Mr Fairlie quite reasonably argued that no-one would have known where the S.N.P. stood if a majority of S.N.P. candidates had been elected in 1983.

The renewed influence of the gradualist left was apparent, however, with conference decisions reflecting a very even division of opinion between fundamentalists and gradualists. While the C.S.A.-inspired resolution calling for an anti-Conservative electoral pact was defeated, the resolutions supporting the establishment of a constitutional convention and participation in the C.S.A. were passed by very narrow majorities.[7] The left also gained ground in the elections to the N.E.C., with Jim Sillars, Kenny MacAskill and Alex Salmond all securing election. There was support for the miners and, significantly, a call for a draft 'workers' charter'. Although not adopted on this occasion, such a charter was included in the 1987 election manifesto. The narrowness of these victories meant that these changes were not yet on a secure footing. As the party president, Donald Stewart, remarked in reference to the pro-C.S.A. resolution, 'I am quite sure that there will be a motion before next year's conference to overturn it'.[8]

While the Inverness conference had redressed the balance between fundamentalists and gradualists somewhat, the S.N.P. was not playing the leading role in any nascent coalition. Labour had already claimed the title by committing itself to participation in the C.S.A., and thereby to a constitutional convention, well in advance of the S.N.P. decision. Somewhat prophetically, there was residual opposition in the S.N.P. to a convention when an N.E.C. paper put forward options early in 1985 on how a convention might be established.[9] The same patterns of organisational behaviour which typified the party's handling of the devolution issue in the 1970s were thus starting to assert themselves, and it was fortunate for the Nationalists that a convention was not established at the time.

There was a marked reduction in factional activity when the party conference convened at Paisley in September 1985. The left consolidated its gains on 'class' issues, much to the disappointment of traditionalists like Donald Stewart who argued that such issues had no place in the S.N.P., while the traditionalists secured majorities against any renewed campaigns of civil disobedience and non-cooperation. There was little open disagreement on the question of independence however. The more pragmatic position taken in 1984 was quietly endorsed by default. Gains for the traditionalists in the elections for national office bearers were balanced by a clean sweep for the left in the elections to the N.E.C.

If the conference appeared a little dull to commentators, the S.N.P.'s campaign in the Regional Council elections in 1986 confirmed that the party was now concentrating on its greater effectiveness than Labour as a Scottish 'pressure group' on social and economic issues. In this context, the S.N.P. paraded two Labour defectors to the media on the eve of the Labour Party's Scottish Conference in March. While they were hardly as prominent as had been intimated beforehand, the S.N.P. claimed that there were many more Labour Party members on the brink of defection. Whether this was accurate or not, the clear intention was to play on the ever-present fear in Labour's ranks of an S.N.P. revival and steer Labour in a nationalist direction. Secondly, the campaigns centred on the steel and coal-mining industries showed that the party had returned to the politics of the short-lived industrial strategy of the early 1980s which had attempted to build working-class and trade union support for nationalism. Central to this strategy was the 'defence' of particular industrial groups, with a subsequent linking of the constitutional question to economic well-being. While not a denial of the party's overriding objective, such campaigning nevertheless involved its relegation.

Yet if a fundamentalist backlash was expected, it clearly failed to make any impression at the 1986 annual conference at Dunoon. The platform concentrated its attacks on the Labour Party for being neither as socialist nor as nationalist as its voters wanted, while the traditionalists complained that the S.N.P. had been taken over by the left. The party's approach to the 1987 general election showed a continuation of this trend by trading on the 'Play the Scottish Card' slogan adopted in the autumn. By this means, the S.N.P. attempted to capitalise on the apparent reservoir of goodwill felt towards it by voters of other parties. While putting forward 'a strong policy for independence', which included a 'Worker's Charter' of a 35-hour week, a minimum wage law and the repeal of 'anti-union' laws, the S.N.P. promised to co-operate with other parties to form an anti-Conservative coalition government in the event of a hung parliament, or a Scottish constitutional convention in the event of a Conservative victory.[10] While the commitment to the convention idea was hedged with ambiguity on the conditions for S.N.P. participation, this was not an immediate problem in the heat of the election campaign, and the Nationalists' opponents made nothing of it.

In attempting to add to Labour's discomfort, Gordon Wilson predicted a Conservative victory in the last week of the campaign and announced that the S.N.P. was switching its effort fully onto the Labour vote. Picking up on the wilder statements issuing from some Labour candidates, the S.N.P. proposed an anti-Thatcher coalition to pursue parliamentary and extra-parliamentary 'action' in the event of the 'constitutional crisis' predicted by George Galloway and others.[11]

The arrival of the so-called 'Doomsday' scenario provoked very little in the way of immediate action from the Nationalists. Content to observe Labour's accelerated drift towards nationalism, the S.N.P. leadership simply buttressed the opening to the left, consolidated the new policy of 'Independence within the European Community' and waited for an opportunity to reap the harvest sown for it by Labour and its allies. Indeed, antipathy between the Labour Party in Scotland and the Nationalists was never far from the surface in spite of their apparent unity in indigation at Mrs Thatcher's third electoral victory. Despite an invitation, the S.N.P. did not participate in the Labour and S.T.U.C.-sponsored 'Festival for Scottish Democracy' held in Glasgow in September 1987, largely because of Labour's insistence at controlling the event.

This made no difference to the solidity of the left's position within the S.N.P., however, as was apparent when the party conference assembled later in the month. Publishing what amounted to a manifesto a few days before the conference convened,[12] nationalist fundamentalists sought to reinstate independence as the party's overriding goal and reverse the leftward drift. Despite protests from Gordon Murray at the conference that the leadership has censored the debate, the fundamentalists were decisively defeated by a margin of four to one, and went on to sustain further defeats on the key issues.

In the debate on the introduction of the government's community charge, for example, the party decided that it would support a popular campaign of non-payment and challenged the Labour party to use its majorities in local government and among Scottish M.P.s to defeat the introduction of the tax. In essentially recognising the legitimacy of Labour's Scottish 'mandate', the latter was particularly offensive to the fundamentalists. A further victory for the left came in the defence debate where, in line with Labour's policy, the conference committed the S.N.P. to a non-nuclear and non-NATO stance. Finally, the figure identified as the architect of the left's gradualist strategy, the newly-elected M.P. for Banff and Buchan, Alex Salmond, was elected as deputy leader of the party, defeating Jim Fairlie in the process. Gordon Wilson's supplications to the party to be realistic and not to try to compete with Labour 'on the far left of the political spectrum'[13] have to be seen in this context. When the conference ended, the fundamentalists had sustained a string of defeats, and in a remarkable reversal of the position in 1982, were now portrayed as the disruptive minority faction.

The decision to mount a campaign of opposition to the community charge was particularly significant, as it subsequently became (along with unemployment), the most important single issue for Scottish voters.[14] In many ways, it parallels the oil campaign of the 1970s, as it can readily be made into a sectional issue which causes discomfort to the major parties. Labour nationally cannot really endorse a mass campaign of non-payment given its wish to resume governing at Westminster at some time in the future, and indeed has not done so. Such a campaign would also be difficult for the party in Scotland, as Labour-controlled local authorities are required to implement the tax if they wish to continue in office. As neither of these caveats apply to the S.N.P., the party has been able to develop further its campaign against the introduction of the community charge and position itself as the most militant opponent of the tax, while enjoying the spectacle of division within Labour's ranks. At the 1988 annual conference held at Inverness, delegates overwhelmingly endorsed a coalitional campaign of non-payment designed to recruit 100,000 non-payers. The few speakers against this return to civil disobedience were greeted with open hostility, while Jim Sillars, supporting the call for the campaign, received a standing ovation.

On this issue, the S.N.P. has been greatly helped by the disarray within the Labour Party and the incompetence with which the Labour leadership has handled its own strategy. Seemingly oblivious to the timing of the S.N.P.'s annual conference, Labour convened a special conference on the 'poll tax' in Glasgow on the day after proceedings had finished in Inverness. While it was apparent that many Labour activists and Scottish Labour M.P.s supported a campaign of non-payment, the Labour leadership had signalled well in advance that the party could not officially endorse such a campaign. It was thus no surprise that S.N.P. delegates at Inverness took the opportunity to exploit this division, taunt Labour M.P.s and throw down the gauntlet of an S.N.P.-supported campaign of non-payment to them. As may have been predicted, Labour's recall conference at Govan was hopelessly divided, and although the official line was endorsed, self-styled Labour rebels pledged to continue to support non-payment. The subsequent formation of the 'Committee of 100' non-payers comprised essentially of Labour and trade union activists, and its incarnation at the local level in the form of anti-poll tax federations is a measure of the S.N.P.'s good fortune and Labour's division.

As if this was not enough, the whole episode coincided with the run-up to the Govan by-election occasioned by Neil Kinnock's nomination of the sitting M.P., Bruce Millan, for one of the vacant European Commissioners' posts. Having seen the confusion at the recall conference, the S.N.P. was able to nominate Jim Sillars as its prospective parliamentary candidate and enjoy the spectacle of another byzantine Labour selection process which produced a candidate who was probably even less appropriate for the circumstances than Harry Selby had been in 1973. Labour's nominee obligingly supported the S.N.P.'s policy of non-payment of the community charge, and produced his most bumbling media performance on the eve of the poll. Needing a swing of just over 27% to unseat Labour, the S.N.P. achieved a swing of 33%, gained 50% of the poll and a majority of three and half thousand over Labour.

If the S.N.P. has capitalised on opposition to the community charge, it has made equally big play of its policy of 'independence within the European Community'. These two themes have dominated S.N.P. campaigning at the Govan and Glasgow Central by-elections, and at the European elections in 1989, although with varying effect. The 'new' policy on Scottish membership of the E.C. is in fact by no means new, as its principal architect Jim Sillars has tirelessly pointed out. Thus, it cannot be the case that its appearance turned the tide for the S.N.P. Ignored and unloved for the first five years of its existence, even its initial adoption did not prove easy. At the 1983 annual conference, Gordon Wilson argued that the S.N.P. should support 'Scottish' membership of the European Community, as this would allow the 'move to independence (to) take place smoothly and easily'.[15] Traditionally, the S.N.P. had always opposed membership of the Community on the grounds that there was no 'Scottish mandate' for it. The logic of the new position was that a future independent Scotland would accept a membership of the Community negotiated while Scotland was still part of the U.K. A heresy to fundamentalists, such a policy inevitably became entangled in the debate between different factions in the party.

By 1986 however, the new policy was conventional wisdom according to Jim Sillars. In the campaign for the Regional Council elections, he argued that the S.N.P. had 'redefined its policy to take account of the reality of the European Community . . . the basic thrust is now towards independence within that Community'.[16] The party's official campaign in the 1987 general election supported this position, and it has been re-endorsed by party conferences subsequently. Both Gordon Wilson and Jim Sillars have remarked that this formula lays to rest the bogey of separatism once and for all, and it is best seen in this light rather than as a well-worked-out practical policy (which it may or may not be as well). In seeming to allay fears agout the radical changes which independence would involve, it is a reformulation of that older, well-known wish for 'independence within the U.K.' – a position now adopted by the Labour Party, ironically.

Whether the policy is well-founded or not (an issue which will be given special consideration in the final chapter), there is no denying its strategic significance for the party's European election campaign. Attempting to link concern over the poll tax and the apparent majority support for a campaign of non-payment with the popularity of the new independence formula, the S.N.P. argued that the Euro-elections would act as a 'referendum' on its own policies, serve as a basis for the allocation of Convention seats and determine the nature of the Scottish 'mandate' which might inform that body.

In the context of the poll evidence and Labour's control of the Convention, such a strategy was only likely to be partially successful. As far as representation in the Convention is concerned, it would have been interesting to see what, if anything, would have happened if the S.N.P. had drawn level or overtaken Labour at the Euro-elections, but this was never likely to happen in any case. While voters seemed to quite like the S.N.P.'s policy on Europe if asked about constitutional 'options', neither the E.C. nor devolution/independence were the major issues for voters at the Euro-elections, or for that matter, at the Glasgow Central by-election. Other than the poll tax, domestic U.K. matters (the

National Health Service, unemployment, inflation) dominated the list of 'most important issues' according to the June *Scotsman*/MORI poll.[17] As in the past, S.N.P. priorities were not completely shared by the voters. The S.N.P. is still linked with the constitutional issue, while Labour nationally is widely seen as the party which defends the health service and is concerned about unemployment.

Given the national context of the Euro-elections and, by implication, the Central by-election, Labour's Scottish campaign was always likely to benefit from these positive associations of its strengths with voters' concerns. Even the S.N.P.'s exploitation of Labour's ambiguous position on the poll tax was not necessarily going to produce benefits for the Nationalists. The registration for and payment of the tax by the vast majority of Scots shows that there is public ambivalence and apprehension about actually breaking the law, and belies expressed support for campaigns of non-payment. In such circumstances, gaining 25·6% of the Euro-vote and 30·2% of the vote in Glasgow Central was a considerable achievement for the S.N.P., although it was undoubtedly helped by the defection of disillusioned centre party voters to Nationalist ranks.

The campaign also side-stepped (temporarily at least), any renewed consideration of the devolution issue, which in the context of the party's absence from the constitutional convention, has continued to be problematic. Indeed, the latter shows that the balance sheet has not been completely positive from the gradualist point of view. The two possible routes identified in 1987 to participation in the convention, (either by direct election or by assembling elected Westminster M.P.s etc.), seemed to epitomise the new spirit of pragmatism abroad in S.N.P. ranks. However, when negotiations to set up the Convention started early in 1989, the S.N.P. decided that it would only participate on the basis of a direct electoral mandate based on proportional representation. Buoyed up by the apparent popularity of the 'independence in Europe' policy and the post-Govan glow, the party's negotiators argued that the June Euro-elections would provide the ideal opportunity to apportion representation on this basis.

The N.E.C.'s decision by a crushing margin of 22 votes to 1 to support this position could not mask the fact that both party activists and S.N.P. voters were divided over the issue. Survey evidence pointed to a 2–1 split in favour of the leadership position in advance of the N.E.C. meeting in February, although the subsequent National Council meeting in March endorsed the N.E.C. stand by a margin of 191 votes to 41.[18] Nevertheless, a third of one of the samples thought that the party's standing would be damaged as a result, and a 'System Three' survey published at the end of March showed that 51% of S.N.P. voters thought that the party was wrong not to take part.[19] Opinion surveys since have shown evidence of an erosion of S.N.P. support and the decision has been widely interpreted as a defeat for the left of the party.

The Tartanising of the Labour Party

As we have argued, the new separatist coalition only exists by virtue of the transformation of Labour in Scotland since 1979. Above all else, this has been an ideological transformation, which has begun latterly to produce organisational consequences for the Labour Party, and for the Scottish and U.K. political systems. While it can be argued that the official reaffirmation of a commit-ment to devolution (but a considerably stronger devolution at that), by the party in 1982, 1983 and 1987 was largely symbolic, this ignores the sea-change in ideas that was taking place at the same time. This being the case, we shall trace through the changes at the level ideas and leave a consideration of the wider consequences until later.

Perhaps the single most important element in this process has been the acceptance by Labour of the idea of the Scottish mandate. As George Reid argued in 1976, this notion is central to the nationalist position on devolution. For nationalists, political sover-eignty is vested in the people of Scotland rather than in Parliament, or indeed any Scottish Assembly which may come into existence. In the 1970s, the Scottish mandate justified S.N.P. support for a half-way house on the grounds that it as what the people seemed to want while reserving the right to extend the powers of a devolved Assembly if there was such a demand from 'the people'. Moreover, the juxtaposing of the Scottish mandate to the idea of Parliamentary sovereignty acted as a consistent ideological challenge to a cor-nerstone of the British constitution.

Given this pedigree, Labour's conversion to the idea of the Scottish mandate must rank as one of the more spectacular examples of its revisionism. The more recently discussed 'dual mandate' strategy is not its origin, however. That is merely an articulation of a position which Labour politicians have been taking for some time. The precedent is to be found in the very expedient that was supposed to 'dish' the nationalists in the first place – the referendum on the Scotland Act of March 1979. Undoubtedly effective as the final coup which demoralised the S.N.P., it also reinforced, indeed legitimised, the idea of the sovereign Scottish mandate. Labour politicians have felt increasingly comfortable with this idea despite its nationalist origins and its profound constitutional implications.

It has found its principal expression in the view that the Conservatives have no mandate to govern Scotland, and that by implication, the mandate is held either by Labour exclusively or by all the opposition parties collectively. In 1983, a group of M.P.s including John Maxton, George Foulkes, John Home-Robertson, Dennis Canavan and David Marshall claimed that since almost three-quarters of the Scottish electorate had voted for parties committed to devolution, the Conservative government had no authority to implement policies in Scotland. This general approach was reflected in Labour's 'Green Paper' published in September 1984 which represented official party policy and the views of the Scottish Trades Union Congress and the Scottish Co-operative Party. Adopting the premise of the S.N.P.'s 'Scotland said Yes' campaign after March 1979, this stated that the 'people of Scotland recorded a clear vote in favour of the Assembly' in the Scotland Act referendum, and advocated a strong assembly with revenue-raising and other powers additional to the 1978 Scotland Act.[20]

Following the 1987 general election, the Scottish press chose to cast Labour in the role of trustee of the mandate. The *Glasgow Herald* declared that 'the Labour victory adds up to a convincing Scottish mandate . . . the case for devolution was both implicit in the result and enhanced by it. . . The Labour Party now finds itself in a sense the custodian of the devolution consensus and will be expected to advance the cause'.[21] In September 1987, the party's Annual Conference congratulated the party in Scotland on winning fifty seats, recognising this as a mandate for a Scottish Assembly, and called upon it to produce a draft devolution bill. The press launch of Labour's Scotland Bill in November 1987 duly justified the bill in terms of the mandate given by the 75% of Scottish voters had supported pro-devolutionary parties at the 1987 general election.

Labour has done much to embellish the concept of the Scottish mandate. According to Donald Dewar, an assembly would have protected the Scottish people 'from much damaging legislation which does not reflect Scottish priorities'.[22] The latter phrase refers to the widely held view in the Labour party that Scotland is naturally a socialist nation which would never on its own elect a Conservative majority. Labour M.P. Norman Hogg remarked recently that Labour had 'defended traditions that have their roots deep in Scottish history and are reflected in the deeply held Scottish conviction that the sick, the poor and the disabled are our collective responsibility'.[23] Based on as selective a reading of historical events as Mrs Thatcher's recent discovery that the Scots invented 'Thatcherism' and are naturally 'Thatcherist', this dimension of the Scottish mandate is buttressed by the vagaries of the electoral system which produces enormous Labour majorities in Scotland, despite the fact that the Conservatives are the only party to have received over 50% of the Scottish vote in modern times (in 1955).

As Drucker has argued, the supposed prevalence of socialism in Scotland was the leitmotif behind the formation of the breakaway Scottish Labour Party in 1976.[24] It may have been the failure of that venture which defused any seccessionist tendencies in the Labour Party at the time, but with the rise of the Salmond–Sillars leadership faction in the S.N.P. and the growing fissures in the Labour Party in Scotland on the national question, such an eventuality is increasingly likely in the 1990s. As far as 'socialism in one country' is concerned, the S.N.P. has merely followed what has become the conventional wisdom in the Labour Party of the 1980s. The only difference is that where Labour see a radical form of devolution as the vehicle to translate socialist will into action, the S.N.P. argue that only independence will achieve this.[25] But by emphasising the negative consequences of Westminster government for Scotland, while raising expectations about the power of a Scottish Assembly to arrest or reverse them, Labour spokesmen are effectively undermining Parliament and promoting the S.N.P.'s case that greater independence from Westminster is the solution to Scotland's problems.

The acceptance of nationalist arguments by Labour does not stop at the theory of the Scottish mandate or its incarnation as the dual mandate however. There is a range of ideological preconceptions, policies and strategies which Labour has inherited from the S.N.P. and earlier nationalist Home Rule movements. The case for devolution has been underpinned by allusions to Scotland's loss of statehood in 1707. Writing in *Radical Scotland*, Jack McConnell, a Stirling District councillor and Labour's prospective parliamentary candidate in Perth and Kinross in 1987, argued that Labour's devolution campaign should show voters 'that the control over their own lives, which Scots have been deprived of for almost three centuries, can be re-established'.[26] In the view of Dennis Canavan MP, 'the people of Scotland did not give their democratic consent to the Act of Union', and the C.S.A.'s 'Blueprint for Scotland' opens its case for an Assembly with the Act of Union, the existence of separate Scottish laws and institutions and a 'feeling of community which characterises a nation'.

Prominent Labour Party figures have also taken up the S.N.P.'s argument that Scotland is a semi-colony. For example, in 1981 Henry Drucker claimed that 'we are fed up with seeing our laws and our customs overruled as if we were some forgotten colony'.[27] After the general election of 1987, John Maxton MP hoped that Mrs Thatcher would 'not try imposing a semi-colonial administration on Scotland', while Dennis Canavan was already sure that Scotland was 'being treated worse than a colony' with the Secretary of State behaving 'like a colonial governor-general'.[28]

In the absence of a commitment by the government to establish a Scottish Assembly, Labour has advocated plans of action similar to those proposed by the S.N.P. in the 1970s, and rejected by Labour at the time. First, Labour now supports various forms of all-party action including the establishment of an interim assembly and/or constitutional convention. By both necessity and choice the party has been at the forefront of actually establishing such a body, rather than simply supporting the idea. Just before the 1983 general election, George Galloway, former chairman of the Labour party in Scotland, was urging the Labour Party and the S.T.U.C. 'to organise a representative Scottish convention which would debate and agree the tactical and strategic paths the campaign for devolution should take . . . such a convention could take on the character of a representative Assembly itself with the Scottish M.P.s of all parties leading the fight'.[29]

While this idea was officially rejected at the time, the decision was reversed at the Labour Party conference in October 1983, and in February 1984, the executive of the Scottish Council of the Labour Party urged constituency Labour Parties, affiliated trade unions and individual Party members to participate in the all-party C.S.A. At the same time, this body produced a discussion document entitled 'The Scottish Constitutional Convention'. In the event of the government rejecting proposals emanating from the Convention, Scottish M.P.s who supported them would constitute an 'Interim Scottish Assembly' which could 'call an election in Scotland on terms of the constitution for Scotland as proposed by the Constitutional Convention'. This was precisely the strategy advocated by the S.N.P., and rejected by the Labour government, when the Scotland and Wales Bill was abandoned in 1977.

A modified plan resurfaced in 1987, when it was suggested that the 'Interim assembly' should also comprise representatives of trade unions, local authorities, the churches and other groups. This was endorsed in every detail by Dennis Canavan one month before the June election. While such views may be expected from Mr Canavan, he is now in influential company. In August 1987, Robin Cook, erstwhile opponent of devolution and a Labour front bench spokesman currently, urged Labour M.P.s in Scotland to set up an alternative forum to Westminster 'somewhere in Scotland, and invite the M.P.s of other parties to join us there and vote on the Scottish issues'.[30] This opportunity was seized both by the S.N.P. and the C.S.A. Gordon Wilson of the S.N.P. immediately declared his party willingness to participate in this 'prototype assembly', and the Campaign subsequently established a panel of '17 prominent Scots' to report on the best way to establish an all-party constitutional convention. Since Govan, Mr Cook has repeated this call and the Labour party is now a full participant in the convention established in March 1989.

At a fringe meeting of the 1988 annual conference of the Scottish Council of the Labour Party, a number of party activists supported by several M.P.s decided that the Party leadership was not doing enough to wrest an assembly from the government, and set up a ginger group, Scottish Labour Action (S.L.A.), which has been instrumental in promoting the dual mandate strategy and setting the agenda for the constitutional convention. Supporting the more forceful tactics long advocated by Dennis Canavan and others, one of the new intake of Labour M.P.s, John McCallion, remarked in June that 'we need the interim assembly to focus anger and pressure on what is undoubtedly an alien and increasingly isolated form of rule'.[31]

Such tactics have long been in the offing. In 1983, George Galloway proposed that Scottish Labour M.P.s should mount a 'full-blown effort at Parliamentary disruption' along the lines pursued by supporters of Irish Home Rule in the earlier part of the century if the government voted a Home Rule bill down. This would be accompanied by selective industrial action and demonstrations in Scotland and a policy of non-cooperation by Scottish local authorities with St Andrew's House.[32]

Other measures proposed by M.P.s to thwart the government included the holding of a plebiscite and the withholding of tax revenues. Just three days after the general election of June 1987, the executive of the Scottish Council of the Labour Party agreed a programme of parliamentary and extra-parliamentary action to force the government to set up a Scottish Assembly, and the 1987 annual conference of the Labour Party in Brighton endorsed the proposal that Labour M.P.s and local authorities should obstruct government legislation if the latter rejected a Scottish Devolution bill. Constructing a similar scenario, Dennis Canavan argued that Labour 'should be prepared to mount a campaign inside and outside Parliament designed to maximise pressure on Westminster . . . (and) take our campaign to the people'.[33] Campbell Christie, the general secretary of the S.T.U.C. described the Conservatives as an 'unrepresentative rump', and said that if the government did not grant Home Rule 'there will have to be parliamentary and extra-parliamentary activity . . . we are prepared for a long period of attrition', while George Foulkes, M.P., warned Malcolm Rifkind 'that we can create problems for him both inside and outside Parliament' if an Assembly was not set up.[34] In addition to the convention, a new 'initiative' came from the Labour-controlled Convention of Scottish Local Authorities (C.O.S.L.A.). Reacting to the Govan result, C.O.S.L.A. has been looking into the possibilities of sponsoring a referendum on the setting up of a Scottish Assembly in order to give it legitimacy – in other words, a 'mandate' from the people.

In the substantive area of the powers and functions of any devolved assembly, Labour has moved towards the S.N.P.'s position of the 1970s. The most significant changes from the provisions of the Scotland Act concern revenue raising and economic powers. Thus, in Labour's 1983 general election manifesto, the Assembly was to have a 'major role in assisting in the regeneration of Scottish industry', and was to have tax raising powers so as to ensure 'that the level of services provided can be determined in Scotland'. The party's U.K. manifesto for 1987 promised a Scottish Assembly 'in the first Parliamentary session' with economic, industrial and tax raising powers, which in all fundamentals was the same as the package put forward by the S.N.P. after the general election of February 1974. Included in Labour's plan was the wish to retain all 72 Scottish M.P.s and the post of Secretary of State for Scotland in the U.K. Cabinet, a position consistently taken by the S.N.P. during the 1970s.

In November 1987, the Labour Party in Scotland went a step further when it published a new Scotland Bill. It stated that although further decentralisation of government to Wales and the English regions might follow, 'Scotland . . . cannot wait for this process . . . (as it) is a distinct nation with its own history, culture, church and law'. The proposed Assembly would have 144 members, who would be elected for a fixed four-year term unless two thirds of their number voted for earlier dissolution. Dual membership of the Westminster Parliament and the Assembly would be allowed, with no reduction in the number or the rights of Scottish M.P.s at Westminster. The Assembly would have control over all the Scottish Office functions prescribed in the 1978 Scotland Act, and additionally would be responsible for the universities, manpower and training, forestry and the police. It would have increased economic powers, including control over the Scottish Development

Agency, the Highlands and Islands Development Board and the electricity industry, and would take over the powers of industrial intervention currently exercised by Westminster. While a central block grant would provide most of the finance, the Assembly would acquire the power to vary the rate of income tax in Scotland. As in the Scotland Act, it would be able to impose, alter or abolish any local government tax including the community charge.

These are substantial additions to what was considered prudent by the last Labour government. Set in the context of the other developments we have outlined, it might have been expected that these proposals would have provoked serious conflict between pro- and anti-devolutionists as in 1978. Yet this has not happened. Since 1979, the party's decision making bodies have become increasingly dominated by devolutionists. In 1984 Donald Dewar remarked that 'certainly within the Labour Party there are no longer any arguments about the need for devolution . . . I cannot think of any subject where the party is more united than on the basic principle of devolution'.[35]

This complacency has now been shaken, but not by Unionist opponents of devolution within the Scottish party. They simply do not exist any longer. Rather, it is the S.N.P. and Labour's own separatists who have provoked the split. The S.L.A. and its supporters are openly at odds with the parliamentary leadership on the question of the dual mandate and the possible withdrawal of Scottish Labour M.P.s from Westminster in the eventuality of a fourth Conservative victory in 1991/2. But it is not simply an argument between the Shadow Secretary and a few activists in the S.L.A. It is now common to hear the Scottish party described as divided between Unionist and nationalist 'wings', a split which extends from the parliamentary party downwards. Indeed, apparent frustration with the Labour leadership has resulted in the formation of yet another separatist organisation – the Scottish Socialist Party – constituted in large part of former Labour activists.

It is significant that the 'option' of Scottish independence within the E.C. gained prominence as a result of the simultaneous utterances of leading figures in the Labour Party (John Pollock), and the S.N.P. (Jim Sillars) As older M.P.s who have had some experience of office at Westminster are gradually replaced, it is likely that this trend will continue. Already few in number, former Scottish Office ministers in the Wilson/Callaghan governments Alex Eadie and Harry Ewing have already announced their retirals, with others likely to follow as the reselection process gets underway. Scottish Labour M.P.s will forget the real constraints which operate on all governments and will turn increasingly to the idea of a Scottish assembly, and then independence, as a means of achieving 'socialism in one country'. Indeed, they already have.

It can be argued that if the Labour Party chose to adopt a more proactive strategy which accorded with its own policy strengths, then it might be able to exploit the divisions within the S.N.P. However, there is absolutely no likelihood of this while Labour continues to plough the nationalist furrow. By choosing to follow the agenda which has been set for them, Labour politicians will insulate the Nationalists from the most destructive consequences of internal debate.

Explaining the Coalition

If the new separatist coalition is primarily the result of changes in the Labour Party, then it is Labour's nationalism which is the more interesting object of explanation rather than the S.N.P.'s pragmatism and socialism. The latter, as we have argued, is based on a determined effort to displace the Labour Party from its position of pre-eminence by confronting it in its urban heartlands. The literature suggests three basic models which might be appropriate explanations for the former however: the office seeking model based on the 'rational choice' perspective, Hechter's (1975) 'internal colonialist' model, and the decline of ideology model based loosely on Bell (1973) and Inglehart (1977).

In the office seeking model, the exploitation of ethnic cleavages results from career self-interest. As Rabushka and Shepsle (1972) suggest, politicians will exploit such divisions if they perceive that they will gain from them.[36] In this particular case, it can be argued that preclusion of Labour from power at Westminster has generated a search for alternative career outlets. This may explain the increased interest in local government generally and, in the case of Scottish Labour M.P.s, aspirant M.P.s and other career politicians in the Labour party in Scotland, an elected assembly. However, if this was the only reason then we would expect Labour politicians concentrated in other areas to find an autonomist dogma of their own.

One coherent explanation of Labour's nationalism is provided by Hechter's model of 'internal colonialism' in the U.K. where, it will be recalled, Hechter argues that nationalism in the Celtic fringes has traditionally been expressed via a disproportionate anti-Conservative vote.[37] While Hechter's own data has been criticised on this score, at least the past two general election results must provide strong circumstantial support for his thesis. If this is the case, then it would not be surprising that Labour became a repository of Scottish nationalism after a long 'centralist' phase. It can further be argued that the ideological transformation of the party is being aided and abetted by the existence of 'inter-active' ethnic cleavages as Hechter and Levi (1977) term them.[38] In this model, certain occupations and institutions are segmented by ethnicity, and thus exist as discreet, ethnically monolithic structures. In Scotland, key opinion-forming groups and occupations such as the legal profession, the media industry and teachers are segmented from their English counterparts, and have arguably provided some of the most vociferous support for nationalism and devolution.

In the ideology model, the decay of class-based philosophies and the advent of post-industrial values, rather than economic disadvantages in the 'periphery' as in Hechter's model, result in a re-ordering of the political agenda by voters. As we have seen, there is insufficient evidence to support the replacment of class-based allegiances by other values among Scottish voters. However, if this model is adapted to refer to ideological change within parties rather than among voters, then Labour's nationalism can co-exist with an electorate which has not in fact become 'nationalist'.

It can be argued that anti-Conservative, and in particular Labour, voting in Scotland has less to do with nationalism than with the relatively greater dependence of Scots on jobs, benefits, services and housing provided by the state. In these circumstances, high support for the party identified with the defence of the public sector is also quite predictable. Allied to this is the idea that the dominant political culture in Scotland is essentially a working-class conservatism resistant to change, which eschews the 'middle-class' values of the southern English (identified with Mrs Thatcher). It is perhaps significant that support for total independence tends to be highest among socio-economic groups D and E and lowest among groups A and B.[39] Thus, support for Labour (and the S.N.P. in the case of Labour defectors), may be principally based upon a dislike of the Conservatives' anti-statist policies rather than their unionism. That Labour's advocacy of devolutionary nationalism is also statist does not make it any the less nationalistic however.

If this is the case, then both the Labour Party and the S.N.P. could be mixing a very dangerous cocktail based on nationalist and statist ideologies. As many have observed, whatever the differences at the elite level, there is a substantial degree of commonality at the membership level and at voter level which could be significant in the light of possible developments which are examined in the final chapter.

Although perhaps for different reasons, it is noteworthy that the S.N.P.'s 'elder statesmen' such as Gordon Wilson and retiring President Donald Stewart have warned against the politics of 'metooism' with Labour. Arguably, the S.N.P.'s recent history shows that the flirtation with 'socialism' is only a temporary phenomenon which, like Labour's commitment to devolution, can be jetisoned as circumstances demand. Despite the apparently comprehensive victory of the pro-devolutionists in the mid-1970s, the traditionalists in the S.N.P. were able to regain control in 1979, and in so far as the party retains a strong non-urban base, the appeal of 'socialism' will always be less than total.

But past precedent is no necessary guide to the future. If, as we have argued, it will be very difficult for Labour to ditch devolution, it may be equally difficult for the S.N.P. to pull back from statism. Only time will tell whether the current orientation of the party, and the dominance of the left on the non-constitutional issues (if not always the consitutional ones), is anything more than an elongated blip.

Notes

[1] T. Dalyell, *Devolution: The End of Britain*, London, Cape, 1977, p. 43. See also H. M. Drucker and G. Brown, *The Politics of Nationalism and Devolution*, London, Longman, 1980, pp. 82–83.

[2] See article by Murray Ritchie in the *Glasgow Herald*, 4 May 1987.

[3] The System Three opinion poll surveys in the *Glasgow Herald* have rated S.N.P. support at 30% in December 1988, 32% in January 1989, 28% in February 1989 and 27% in March. Other polls have tended to give the S.N.P. slightly lower support, with the *Scotsman*/MORI poll for March rating it 24% and the *Scotland on Sunday*/B.B.C. On the Record/MORI poll rating it at 20%.

[4] *Glasgow Herald*, 21 May 1983, and R. Parry, *Scottish Political Facts*, Edinburgh, T. & T. Clark, 1988, Table 1.3, p. 5.

[5] See reports in the *Glasgow Herald*, and *The Guardian*, 25 February 1985.

[6] *Glasgow Herald*, 7 June 1983.

[7] The motion supporting the constitutional convention was endorsed by 246 votes to 238, and the pro-C.S.A. motion was passed by 182 votes to 174. See *Glasgow Herald*, 15 September 1984.

[8] *Glasgow Herald*, 15 September 1984.

[9] *Glasgow Herald*, 27 Februrary 1985.

[10] *Glasgow Herald*, 27 May 1987.

[11] *Glasgow Herald*, 6 June 1987, 9 June 1987 and 10 June 1987.

[12] *Glasgow Herald*, 23 September 1987.

[13] *Glasgow Herald*, 24 September 1987.

[14] *Scotsman*, 8 June 1989.

[15] *Glasgow Herald*, 10 October 1983.

[16] *Glasgow Herald*, 21 March 1986.

[17] *The Scotsman*, 8 June 1989. The issues most frequently identified as important by respondents were: the Community Charge/Poll Tax (20%); Unemployment (20%); National Health Service (19%); Inflation (12%), Devolution/Independence was identified as important by 10% and the E.C. by 5%.

[18] See survey in *The Sunday Times*, 12 February 1989, of 61 S.N.P. Constituency Association convenors, and the B.B.C. Left, Right and Centre survey of 94 activists reported in the same source.

[19] S.T.V. System Three survey published in the *Glasgow Herald*, 30 March 1989.

[20] *Devolution: Labour's Green Paper*, Glasgow, The Labour Party, 1984.

[21] *Glasgow Herald*, 13 June 1987.

[22] *Glasgow Herald*, 1 March 1985.

[23] *Glasgow Herald*, 2 November 1987.

[24] H. M. Drucker, *Breakaway: The Scottish Labour Party*, Edinburgh, Edinburgh University Student Publication Board, 1978.

[25] See H. M. Drucker (ed.), *Socialist Arguments for Devolution*, Labour Campaign for a Scottish Assembly, Edinburgh, 1981.

[26] *Radical Scotland*, February/March 1987.

[27] See Drucker, *Socialist Arguments for Devolution*, p. 1.

[28] *The Independent*, 13 June 1987; *Glasgow Herald*, 8 May 1987 and 14 January 1988.

[29] *Glasgow Herald*, 1 June 1983.

[30] *Glasgow Herald*, 31 August 1987.

[31] *Glasgow Herald*, 6 June 1988.

[32] *Glasgow Herald*, 1 June 1983.

[33] *Glasgow Herald*, 8 May 1987.

[34] *The Independent*, 13 June 1987; *Glasgow Herald*, 13 June 1987.

[35] *Glasgow Herald*, 1 March 1984.

[36] A. Rabushka and K. A. Shepsle, *Politics in Plural Societies: A Theory of Democratic Instability*, Ohio, Merrill and Co., 1972.

[37] M. Hechter, *Internal Colonialism: The Celtic fringe in British national development, 1956–1966*, London, Routledge, Kegan and Paul, 1975.

[38] M. Hechter and M. Levi, 'The Comparative Analysis of Ethnoregional Movements', *Ethnic and Racial Studies* 2, 3, 1979, pp. 261–272.

[39] *Glasgow Herald*, 18 October 1987.

CHAPTER 7

Conclusions and Speculations

Whatever mistakes have been made in the past, Nationalists would argue that the future belongs to them. As British politics enters a period of uncertainty in the twilight of the Thatcher era, the 1990s may produce an S.N.P. revival which even exceeds that of the 1970s. In the context of the collapse of the centre parties, Labour's untested ability to deliver and the growing importance of the European Community, increasing numbers of Scottish voters may consider supporting the S.N.P.

The question is, what will the S.N.P. be able to make of these opportunities if and when they arise? From the limited perspective of this study, a number of conclusions suggest themselves which offer some comfort to the S.N.P.'s competitors. The last great revival showed that even when circumstances are favourable, it is extremely difficult for a party of this type to make the transition from 'third' to major party status. While it may be argued that the S.N.P. behaved neither more nor less rationally than its major competitors, its failure to take full advantage, and to minimise damage to itself, resulted in particularly severe electoral and organisational consequences.

On the issue of North Sea/'Scottish' oil, the S.N.P. certainly did behave quite 'rationally'. It sought to develop what was a new segmentally-based issue, and was able to occupy an extremely popular position for a while. Its competitors were put on the defensive because oil transgressed traditional party alignments to reveal a sectional fissure between English and Scots voters. However, in order to undermine the Labour voté, the party had to develop a radical anti-Conservative strategy, and it was only partly successful in doing this. While most of its fire was directed against the incumbent Conservative government, the Labour Party was not immune from attacks either. Perhaps this was inevitable in the context of Labour's essentially unionist perspective on the issue at the time, but as recent developments have shown, Labour can be prised away from its unionism under certain conditions.

The S.N.P.'s strategy was coalitional in the sense that it tried to appeal to Scottish opinion outside of the political parties, much as it is doing now with its 'Independence in the E.C.' strategy. The oil campaign tried to incorporate various interest groups and public bodies into an alliance which reflected the S.N.P.'s perspective. Yet, in spite of the fact that the party's orientation was generally 'rational', the pace and direction of the campaign were inhibited, deflected and ultimately defeated by internal constraints. The original concept of the campaign underwent critical changes in emphasis after the OPEC crisis of 1973 and, particularly, between the two general elections of 1974.

As in the case of oil, the S.N.P. tried to develop a rational, market-oriented approach to devolution. It was even less successful at doing so however. The devolution episode revealed an erratic pattern of behaviour caused by deep-seated ideological pressures and organisational weaknesses which intensified as the issue dragged on. Given that the party had little choice but to address the issue, the rational course of action would have been to moderate its position while trying to minimise the organisational costs involved. In 1974–75, there was every sign that this might be achieved. However, this chance was lost as unresolved ideological objections asserted themselves, and new sources of organisational instability appeared with the creation of the parliamentary group and the expansion of party membership. The S.N.P.'s inability to clarify its own position on devolution meant that it was unable to develop a coalitional strategy, a particularly damaging omission in the circumstances of the referendum in 1979. The pursuit of two contradictory objective simultaneously – accommodating devolution while trying to assuage knee jerk nationalism – resulted in the worst possible outcome. By 1979, the party's competitors had transformed devolution into a partisan issue and relegated the nationalists to the fringes.

At a more general level, it appears that S.N.P. decision-makers were not able to reach a consensus on the meaning of vital 'management' information in the form of opinion survey data. Their input into policy making was marginal therefore, especially as the poll findings became increasingly unfavourable. The inability to face up to reality was symptomatic of the more fundamental orientations which animated the leadership. Office seeking in the Downsian sense arguably never was, and certainly did not remain the dominant motivation within the party leadership. Leadership figures were as much driven by their own preferences, and the competitive pressures within the leadership, as by their desire to hold public office. This is not wholly unexpected even within the parameters of Downs's model however. It can be comfortably predicted that the desire to hold public office will be weakened when there is little perceived likelihood of achieving it. This was certainly the case of many of the party's M.P.s in 1979, and for most prospective candidates over most of the period.

In any case, it can be argued that the pressures away from a 'market' orientation are likely to strengthen relatively between elections as the opportunity for competing for office recedes into the background. Parties can and do fall into very bad habits in these circumstances, as office holders and erstwhile office seekers look more towards their own organisational base than the electorate. It may seem relatively costless for office-holders to secure their ground by indulging activist preferences, but the price of the Dutch auction which inevitably results from this will have to be paid collectively in the form of lost votes at the next election. Reviewing the evidence, one cannot help concluding that this is what happened in the S.N.P. between 1974 and 1979. Rather than maturity augmenting rationality, irrationality and chaos developed out of internal competition instead. If there was a hidden hand regulating the internal 'market' in this case, it did not produce beneficial results.

But this model of what might be termed rationally-induced decrepitude does not quite fit the facts either. The party leaders oriented themselves alternately to the voters, their own supporters and their own preferences, with scant regard for the prevailing state of grass roots 'opinion' within the party. As there was no coherent mechanism for gauging such opinion, the leaders cannot be accused of wilfully ignoring it. The only opinion which counted for anything was manufactured within the confines of the party's decision-making forums.

This was well-illustrated by the S.N.P.'s experience subsequent to 1979, where the leadership factionalised and fragmented, and the party's supporters and members voted with their feet, migrating to the Labour Party and the Alliance in many cases. This constituted the third and final phase of the party's growth cycle, where it turned completely away from electoral concerns and became preoccupied with internal affairs. Indeed, as voters and members were lost and the party's organisational base shrank to its zealot core, the process of recrimination and leadership turnover was always likely to intensify. The task of rebuilding the organisation in such circumstances was inevitably bound to be slow, and so it has proved to be, especially with the entry of a 'new' third party into the arena in 1983 and the temporary hegemony of Labour's all-embracing cosy nationalism.

However, in the best traditions of British politics, the Nationalists have not had to do all the reconstruction work themselves. As we have argued in connection with the Labour Party, one of S.N.P.'s principal competitors has prepared the ground for a nationalist revival by capitulating so convincingly to nationalist arguments. Labour's drift towards nationalism is not the only aspect of the S.N.P.'s recent good fortune. The Nationalists' main competitor in the centre ground has self-immolated in a rather different, but equally effective way. The demise of the S.D.P.–Liberal Alliance since 1987 has helped the Nationalists as much as the Nationalist decline of 1979–82 helped the Alliance. Third party voters who may have deserted the S.N.P. for the Alliance in 1983 and 1987 are returning to the S.N.P. in 1989.

That only leaves the Conservative Party which, given its Unionist credentials, cannot be expected to have contributed much in the way of disaffected partisans to the Nationalist revival. In another sense, there is no doubt that the Thatcher governments since 1979 have contributed substantially to it. This is not simply a reference to Mrs Thatcher's deep unpopularity in Scotland, or the apparent unpopularity of many of her government's policies. The rise in the standard of living of those in work in Scotland has scarcely made any difference to Conservative support, as there is a general predisposition either to discount the existence of the rise altogether or to relegate its importance in favour of other considerations.

In addition to the imposition of a community charge in Scotland in advance of the rest of the U.K., the Conservative contribution to the problem has been a sin of omission. As one election has succeeded another, the disparity between voting patterns and Parliamentary representation has increased, producing enormous Conservative majorities in the south of England and enormous Labour majorities in Scotland, out of all proportion to the votes cast. By refusing to countenance any constitutional reform, the government has simply exacerbated the significance of the disparity. In this context only, both the major parties are in agreement. Neither will consider a reform of the electoral system to iron out these disparities as it would in all likelihood disadvantage them both.

The Conservative government, preoccupied with effecting its social and economic revolution based on the new individualism, has been content to maintain the constitutional status quo. For its own reasons, Labour has been promoting the idea of devolution, now 'home rule' for Scotland instead of pursuing other avenues of constitutional reform. The failure by the big parties to address territorial imbalances in representation in terms other than either supporting or opposing new levels of government, inevitably directs the debate onto ground favourable to the Nationalists. So long as the Labour Party argues that the government has 'no mandate' to govern Scotland and embarks on extra-parliamentary campaigns for devolution, the Nationalists are under little pressure. On the contrary, their work is being done for them. Why have a dog and bark yourself?

For the moment therefore, it matters little whether the Nationalists participate in the Constitutional Convention or not. In any case, they have already had a large influence on the Convention through the formulation of the Claim of Right, the Convention's founding document. The Claim endorses the idea of the sovereignty of the Scottish people which, as we have argued, is at the heart of the nationalist position on devolution, and constitutional change generally for that matter. The opening sentence of the Claim pledges that '(w)e, gathered as the Scottish Constitutional Convention, do hereby acknowledge the sovereign right of the Scottish people to determine the form of government best suited to their needs'.[1]

This document has been signed by the 150 representatives, predominantly Labour Party M.P.s, M.E.P.s and local councillors, who attended the first meeting. As the document also pledges the Convention to campaign for whatever scheme is finally adopted, the Convention is almost inevitably on a collision course with the government which will either ignore or reject what it proposes. In this case, the Convention will have no choice but to assert the sovereignty of the Scottish people. Unless this is just empty rhetoric, then some form of action will have to be taken, of which the withdrawal of Westminster M.P.s to Edinburgh as advocated by the S.N.P. and now the S.L.A. within the Labour Party, may be the very least of what can be expected.

The Claim of Right represents a substantial political coup for the Nationalists which can be cashed in at some future date. In fact, the value of the Claim for the Nationalists may well be strengthened by their absence from the Convention. No-one who signed the document will be able to argue later that they only did so to keep the Nationalists in the Convention or were under pressure from S.N.P. delegates.

As we have suggested, these developments have potentially explosive consequences for Labour which may fragment the party into two separate entities. Such an eventuality can only be applauded by the S.N.P. The constitutional issue has now become an obsession in the Scottish Labour Party. No fewer than 17 resolutions on the subject, only one of which contained any critical reference to the S.N.P., were submitted for discussion at the 74th annual Scottish conference in March 1989. None of them wanted anything less than an assembly, and most of them wanted one to be set up with or without legislation. Indeed, many Labour politicians have already decided that devolution is a 'dead duck'. They have passed judgement on an assembly's effectiveness before one has even been set up. Devolution is in danger of becoming yesterday's policy. Such is the negative image of devolution already that Labour leaders now refer to 'home rule' instead. It can only be a matter of time before that too is superceded by 'independence within the E.C.' or some other formulation.

Since the establishment of the Convention, it is increasingly likely that support for such an option will increase. The 42 Labour M.P.s who attended the Convention and signed the Claim of Right, are now committed formally to the idea of sovereignty of the Scottish people. Any rejection of the Convention's proposals by the government will obligate the Convention to invoke the authority of that sovereign. According to recent survey evidence, if given the choice between the status quo and 'independence in Europe', no less than 61% of the Scottish electorate believe that Scotland would be better off with '(a)n independent Scottish government which was a separate member of the E.C.'[2] By their own hand, the Conventioneers have set themselves on a road to a confrontation with Westminster. Unwilling bed-partner it may be, but the Labour Party will find itself in alliance with the S.N.P. in calling for a referendum on the future government of Scotland in such an eventuality.

Up until Govan, Labour's devolution policy could possibly have been interpreted as a clever double bluff. Anticipating the 1987 Scotland Bill, Amanda Mitchison argued that 'the very act of presenting a bill which makes no compromise over Scottish representation in the House of Commons suggests that Labour's commitment to a Scottish Assembly is largely rhetorical'.[3] This at least endowed Labour with a certain capacity for calculating deception. Govan, however, confirmed that Labour was in a state of continued organisational paralysis and incapable of serious policy development. The report by Joyce Gould to Labour's National Executive revealed shortcomings in the selection and campaigning mechanisms at Govan, which allowed the defence of a safe seat held by a Labour moderate to fall to a candidate supported by Militant Tendency. The much-heralded 1987 'reform' of Labour's selection procedures was so much empty rhetoric in Govan. It is ironic indeed that Mr Sillars owes a debt of gratitude to the 'internationalists' in Militant Tendency who helped select his opponent.

The subsequent appearance of Labour's policy review document, coupled with the warm glow produced by the Euro-election results and the victory of the Labour candidate at Glasgow Central, has resulted in inevitable comparisons with 'the turning of the Nationalist tide' at the Glasgow Garscadden by-election in 1978. That the Glasgow Central result, where the S.N.P. trebled its share of the vote, is seen as a famous victory by Labour itself speaks volumes. The policy review document faces an uncertain future, and nothing changes the fact that Labour and the S.N.P. are still indistinguishable on many policies. More importantly, Labour and S.N.P. voters are perhaps closer on the issues than they have ever been.

Whatever miracles the policy review may achieve for Labour, it does not address the developing strain between the party nationally and the Labour Party in Scotland. The end result of this could be the secession of the Scottish party. Since 1985, the latter is 'semi-detached' insofar as it is allowed to publish a separate general election manifesto, so creating the possibility of incompatibility between the Scottish and British programmes. With the affiliation of many party organisations to the C.S.A. and the setting up of the Convention, this is quite likely to happen on the issue of a future Assembly and the priority it would get from an incoming Labour government. A further sign of organisational fragmentation is the demand for full autonomy for the party in Scotland in drawing up its manifesto and appointing staff.

There are two main aspects of the question of secession, the first of which stems from the Labour majority in Scotland and the attendant issue of the 'Scottish mandate'. In this sense, there has been a question-mark over the relationship between Labour nationally and the Scottish party since 1983. George Foulkes warned then that 'a major realignment in Scottish politics with Labour M.P.s and the trade unions forming a breakaway movement could be possible if the Scottish Labour/Westminster Tory arithmetic were the same after the forthcoming (1983) election'.[4] If this was the case in 1983, then it was even more so in 1987 with the arrival of the 'Doomsday' scenario. In August 1987, *The Times* reported that some fifteen Scottish M.P.s were already contemplating secession from the party nationally if the Conservatives were to win yet another election – or Doomsday 2 as it is becoming known.

The other aspect is rooted in the devolution policy itself which, as became apparent during the passage of the devolution legislation between 1975 and 1979, is deeply unpopular with many English Labour M.P.s. Thus, it is significant that when John Maxton failed in his attempt to introduce a Devolution Bill in Parliament in March 1985, seven Labour M.P.s from the north of England voted with the Conservatives because they believed that English regions such as the North East would be seriously disadvantaged by such a proposal. Perhaps recognising this problem and under pressure from English Labour M.P.s, Neil Kinnock made virtually no reference to devolution when he addressed the Scottish Council of the Party in March 1988, an omission which caused some consternation among delegates. Despite his well-known and frequently expressed distaste for nationalism, Kinnock has reasserted his party's commitment to devolution for Scotland, but it must remain an open question whether any future Labour government could deliver hostile M.P.s for devolution.

The solution now proposed by Roy Hattersley is that all the English regions will get assemblies as well, but this has been opposed by Scottish Labour M.P.s on the grounds that it would slow down the process of self-government for Scotland. If Labour is returned to power at Westminister, then other consequences will follow from its current posturing on devolution. The subscription to the theory of the 'Scottish mandate' inevitably raises questions about Labour's mandate elsewhere in the U.K. It cannot maintain with any consistency that the Conservatives have no mandate to govern Scotland when Labour has governed the U.K. on three occasions since 1964 without a 'mandate' in England. It may argue that the Scottish mandate is based on a different constitutional principle to the mandate in the rest of the U.K., so allowing a Labour government to exercise power in both places for different reasons. This would hardly strengthen Labour's claim to be a party of government representing the whole of the U.K., and would buttress the nationalists' claim of Scottish 'separateness'.

Should devolution for Scotland be introduced by a Labour government with an inevitably thin majority, the disqualification of English, Welsh and Northern Irish M.P.s from voting on Scottish matters would require consideration of applying the same rule to Scottish M.P.s voting on English matters (the 'West Lothian question'). While it is impossible to imagine that a Labour government would willingly introduce such a provision, as it would fear losing its majority, the opposition parties might combine with any dissident Labour M.P.s to support it. The Conservatives would support it as a means of precluding the likelihood of a future

Labour government at Westminster, the Democrats would support it on the grounds that it might increase the possibility of coalition government and the Nationalists would support it as a means of further weakening the Union.

In the eventuality of a minority Labour government at Westminster sustained by the Nationalists and the Democrats, there would be a heavy price to pay. The S.N.P. would demand even more powers for the Assembly, and could combine with the Democrats to force proportional representation (P.R.) for it. At a stroke, Labour's 'natural' majority in any Scottish Assembly would be destroyed. The Democrats have already demanded the introduction of P.R. for the Convention as the price for their continuing participation, and there is now a growing caucus of opinion within the Labour Party itself for P.R. for U.K. elections generally. Over 40 resolutions supporting the introduction of some form of P.R. were submitted to the 1989 Labour Party conference.

Finally, there is the question of local government. Assuming that the Conservative government does not reform it out of existence first, the Scottish system of two tier local government would not in all likelihood survive devolution. The S.N.P. pledged to abolish one tier at the time of the great devolution debate in the 1970s, and it is now generally accepted by Labour politicians that one tier will have to go if a Scottish Assembly is established. Thus, there is the prospect that Labour's local government empire in Scotland, by which the party has set great store nationally, will be dismembered by its own rulers. The leader of Scotland's largest region has already accepted this as an inevitable consequence of devolution.

As for the S.N.P., much is hoped for from the policy of 'Independence within the E.C.' and the party's militant opposition to the community charge. As we have argued, the imposition of the community charge has proved particularly difficult for the Labour Party to handle as it has ambitions to be in government again, and cannot really sanction law breaking. On the other hand, the S.N.P. has few qualms about constitutional improprieties, as it neither aspires to nor has any chance of holding office at Westminster.

Should it gain control of more local authorities however, S.N.P. councillors will find themselves in the invidious position of having to collect the charge, increase it to cover any rises in expenditure, or both in order to stay within the law. The alternatives are to defy the law and face possible surcharge and disqualification, or resign. While the latter options may appear to be preferable to the activists, they are hardly likely to improve the party's image as responsible administrators capable of running a separate country, negotiating international treaties etc. The S.N.P.'s past experience in local government has not been altogether happy, with many attributing the post-1969 dip in support to the poor performance of some new S.N.P. councillors elected in 1968. In this context, there is already open conflict between S.N.P. councillors on Tayside and party headquarters over the issue of the compulsory competitive tendering of cleaning services by that Region. Offered this kind of uncertainty, voters may well choose to stay with the tried and tested major party alternatives.

The policy of 'Independence within the E.C.' has come in for more sustained and coherent criticism by Labour politicians, although this has been fatally weakened by their conversion to the theory of the Scottish mandate. The S.N.P.'s case has been built upon a series of assumptions about rights of entry into the E.C. and co-operation from other member states in securing this. S.N.P. spokesmen argue that as there is no provision for secession in the Community treaties, Scotland would automatically become a full member once independence from the rest of the U.K. had been secured. Citing the case of Greenland's withdrawal as a precedent, it is argued that full statehood is not a precondition for a change in status.

Critics have argued that as it was the U.K. which negotiated its way into the Community, then Scotland would negotiate itself out of the Community when it negotiated its way out of the U.K. While international legal precedent (in the form of the Vienna Convention) does not support this criticism according the S.N.P., the question of independent Scottish membership of the E.C. may have little to do with legal precedent in the final analysis. Musing on the possibility of German reunification and the position of such a state in the E.C., Jim Sillars argues that 'the politics of Europe would dicate the automatic continuation of the new state as a member of the Community'.[5] In other words, where there is a political will there is a way – to block either membership or accept it – irrespective of international legal precedent.

The case of Greenland provides only ambiguous support for the S.N.P.'s case. As the Danish government had to negotiate on behalf of the Greenlanders, the question arises of who would negotiate on behalf of Scotland in the pre-independence phase. The Sillars formula of 'upon attaining an independence mandate, Scotland would enter into negotiation with the U.K. and the Community simultaneously'[6] is hardly a model of clarity. In its breathtaking assumption, it is only exceeded by the assertion that 'a transitional timescale of one year should be ample' for the completion of this process.[7] It took the Greenlanders three years to complete all the negotiations, while Scotland, without an Assembly (which the Greenlanders had), without a government, and wanting full membership of the E.C. and separation from the U.K. all at the same time, is going to complete this in a year.

Secondly, the Greenlanders did not want what the S.N.P. is asking for. They wanted withdrawal from, rather than full sovereignty within the Community with full membership rights. Had Greenland been trying to negotiate the same status that the S.N.P. proposes for Scotland, then the outcome might have been very different. On the assumption that existing member states would be unhappy to preside over their own dismemberment and watch the breakaway states assume separate places at the common table, it can be argued that entry would not be automatic by any means in such cases. Moreover, a Community of 20 or more members would require further institutional and policy reform, as it could not function on its present basis.

The economic basis of the Sillars argument is twofold. On the one hand, E.C. membership will prevent Scotland suffering any economic discrimination as a result of independence, while on the other, independence will enable it to manage its economic destiny in line with national needs. In the context of the Single European Act and its implementation in 1992, it is argued that independence would entail no drastic economic consequences for Scotland, and as a separate state, Scotland would gain full membership rights with representation comparable to the smaller states of Luxembourg, Ireland, Denmark and Greece. At the same time, it is argued that independence would give Scotland 'full control over (its) economy', and enable a Scottish government to block any E.C. policies which 'would prove injurious to Scotland's economic future'.[8] A Scottish government, so it is claimed, will be the only device able to counteract the forces of economic centralisation given added impetus by the Single European Act.

Such arguments are hardly consistent as critics have pointed out. If the Single European Act is to be the economic guarantee of Scotland's transition from a part of the U.K. to an independent state, then it cannot be argued that a Scottish government will be able to circumvent its effects if it does not like them. For the corollary of the latter is that other member states (the remainder of the U.K. for example), will do the same, and the consequences of that are that no single market will exist, and all the guarantees of equal access to markets will be worthless. As every member state government well knows, a genuine single market entails a considerable surrender of sovereignty up to and including a single currency system. Nowhere does the S.N.P. say that a Scottish government would forgo a separate currency and stay within the Sterling system. It must be assumed on the basis of past S.N.P. policy, that there would be a separate Scottish currency. In this case, Scottish businesses in an independent Scotland would not have the free access that they presently have to the rest of the U.K. with all the consequences that is likely to entail. It might be added that such a fragmentation of an existing integrated market is hardly likely to meet with much enthusiasm in Brussels. If there is to be a single market, then the type of economic intervention the S.N.P. is suggesting is simply incompatible with it; if there is not to be a single market, then the S.N.P. is failing to take any account of the likely consequences.

While the appeal of the 'Independence in Europe' may be something of a nine day wonder, this is by no means certain. Arguably, the Constitutional Convention may become the main vehicle for the advancement of this policy if the Greenland precedent is anything to go by. The devolved assembly there played an important part in moving the policy of E.C. withdrawal forward. Thus, while the S.N.P. can remain outside of the Convention in the short term, it cannot afford to stay out indefinitely. Given the response the Convention proposals are likely to get from Mrs Thatcher, the Nationalists may find their opponents already suitably attired for a European adventure if and when they do return.

Notes

1 Reported in the *Glasgow Herald* and *The Independent*, 31 March 1989.
2 *Glasgow Herald*/BBC System Three opinion poll published in the *Glasgow Herald*, 14 April 1989.
3 A. Mitchison, 'Playing Politics with Scotland', *New Society*, 25 September 1987, p. 17.
4 Reported in the *Glasgow Herald*, 1 June 1983.
5 J. Sillars, *Independence in Europe*, Glasgow, June 1989, p. 32.
6 Ibid., p. 30.
7 Ibid.
8 Ibid., p. 6.

Bibliography

ABRAMS, M. (1964) 'Opinion Polls and Party Propaganda' *Public Opinion Quarterly*, 28, pp. 13–19.

AGNEW, J. A. (1981) 'Political Regionalism and Scottish Nationalism in Gaelic Scotland', *Canadian Review of Studies in Nationalism*, 8, 1, pp. 115–130.

ALEXANDER, A. (1980) 'Scottish Nationalism: Agenda Building, Electoral Processes and Political Culture', *Canadian Review of Studies in Nationalism*, 7, 2, pp. 372–385.

ALEXANDER, K. J. W. (1975) *The Political Economy of Change*, Oxford, Blackwell.

BARRY-JONES, J. and KEATING, M. (1979) *The British Labour Party as a Centralising Force*, Glasgow, Centre for the Study of Public Policy.

BAXTER-MOORE, N. (1979) 'The Rise and Fall of the S.N.P.: Revisited', paper delivered to the European Politics Group Workshop, London, Ontario, 17–19 December.

BEGG, H. M. and STEWART, J. A. (1971) 'The Nationalist Movement in Scotland', *Journal of Contemporary History*, 6, 1, pp. 135–152.

BIRCH, A. H. (1978) 'Minority Nationalist Movements and Theories of Political Integration', *World Politics*, 30, 3, pp. 325–344.

BIRCH. A. H. (1979) *Political Integration and Disintegration in the British Isles*, London, Allen and Unwin.

BLEIMAN, D. and KEATING, M. (1979) *Labour and Scottish Nationalism*, London, Macmillan.

BOCHEL, J. and DENVER, D. (1972) 'The Decline of the S.N.P.: An Alternative View', *Political Studies*, 20, 3, pp. 311–316.

BOCHEL, J., DENVER, D. and MACARTNEY, A. (eds.) (1981) *The Referendum Experience: Scotland 1979*, Aberdeen, Aberdeen University Press.

BOGDANOR, V. (1979) *Devolution*, Oxford, Oxford University Press.

BOGDANOR, V. (1981) *The People and the Party System: The Referendum and Political Reform in British Politics*, Cambridge, Cambridge University Press.

BOGDANOR, V. (1982) 'Ethnic Nationalism in Western Europe', *Political Studies*, 30, 2, pp. 284–291.

BRAND, J. (1978) *The National Movement in Scotland*, London, Routledge.

BRAND, J., McLEAN, I., and MILLER, W. (1983) 'The Birth and Death of a Three Party System: Scotland in the Seventies', *British Journal of Political Science*, 13, 4, pp. 463–488.

BRETON, A. (1964) 'The Economics of Nationalism', *Journal of Political Economy*, 72, pp. 376–386.

BROWN, G. (ed.). (1975) *The Red Paper on Scotland*, Edinburgh, Edinburgh University Student Publications Board.

BUDGE, I. and URWIN, D. W. (1966) *Scottish Political Behaviour*, London, Barnes and Noble.

BUDGE, I., BRAND, J., MARGOLIS, M. and SMITH, A. (1972) *Political Stratification and Democracy*, London, Macmillan.

BUDGE, I. and FARLIE, D. (1977) *Voting and Party Competition: A Theoretical Critique and Synthesis Applied to Surveys from Ten Democracies*, London, Wiley.

BUTT-PHILIP, A. (1978) 'Devolution and Regionalism' in COOK, C and RAMSDEN, J. (eds.), *Trends in British Politics since 1945*, London, Macmillan.

CAMPBELL, A., CONVERSE, P., MILLER, W. E. and STOKES, D. (1966) *Elections and the Political Order*, New York, Wiley.

CLARKE, H. D. and ZUK, G. (1989) 'The Dynamics of Third Party Support: The British Liberals 1951–79', *American Journal of Political Science*, 33, 1, pp. 196–221.

COUPLAND, R. (1954) *Welsh and Scottish Nationalism: A Study*, London, Collins.

CRAWFORD, R. M. (1982) 'The S.N.P., 1960–74: An Investigation into Its Organisation and Power Structure', Ph.D. thesis, University of Glasgow.

CURRY, R. L. and WADE, L. L. (1968) *A Theory of Political Exchange: Economic Reasoning in Political Analysis*, New Jersey, Prentice Hall.

CREWE, I., SARLVIK, B. and ALT, J. (1977) 'Partisan Dealignment in Britain 1964–74', *British Journal of Political Science*, 7, 2, pp. 129–190.

CREWE, I. and HARROP, M. (eds.) (1986) *Political Communication and the General Election of 1983*, Cambridge, Cambridge University Press.

DAALDER, H. and MAIR, P. (eds.) (1983) *Western European Party Systems: Continuity and Change*, Beverly Hills, Sage.

DICKSON, T. (1978) 'Class and Nationalism in Scotland', *Scottish Journal of Sociology*, 2, 2, 143–162.

DALYELL, T. (1977) *Devolution: The End of Britain?*, London, Cape.

DELAMONT, S. (1976) 'Cultural Reproduction and Scottish Elites', *Scottish Journal of Sociology*, 1, 1, pp. 29–44.

DEUTSCH, K. A. (1953) *Nationalism and Social Communication: An Enquiry into the Foundations of Nationality*, New York, Wiley.

DOWNS, A. (1957) *An Economic Theory of Democracy*, New York, Harper.

DRUCKER, H. (1978) *Breakaway: The Scottish Labour Party*, Edinburgh, Edinburgh University Student Publications Board.

DRUCKER, H. and BROWN, G. (1980) *The Politics of Nationalism and Devolution*, London, Longman.

DRUCKER, H. and DRUCKER, N. (1980) *The Scottish Government Yearbook 1980*, Edinburgh, Paul Harris.

DUNLEAVY, P. and HUSBANDS, C. T. (1983) *British Democracy at the Crossroads; Voting and Party Competition in the 1980s*, London, Allen and Unwin.

DUVERGER, M. (1954) *Political Parties*, New York, Wiley.

EAGLES, M. (1985) 'The Neglected Regional Dimension in Scottish Ethnic Nationalism', *Canadian Review of Studies in Nationalism*, 12, 1, pp. 81–98.

EDWARDS, O. D. (1968) *Celtic Nationalism*, London, Routledge.

EISENSTADT, S. N. and ROKKAN, S. (1973) *Building States and Nations* (2 vols.) Beverly Hills, Sage.

ELDERSVELD, S. J. (1964) *Political Parties: A Behavioural Analysis*, Chicago, Rand McNally.

EPSTEIN, L. (1967) *Political Parties in Western Democracies*, London, Pall Mall.

ESMAN, M. J. (ed.) (1977) *Ethnic Conflict in the Western World*, New Haven, Cornell.

FROHLICH, N., OPPENHEIMER, J. and YOUNG, O. (1971) *Political Leadership and Collective Goods*, Princeton, Princeton University Press.

FURNIVALL, J. S. (1939) *Netherlands India*, Cambridge, Cambridge University Press.

FUSARO, A. (1979) 'Two faces of British nationalism: The SNP and PC Compared,' *Polity*, 11, 3, pp. 362–386.

GELLNER, E. (1969) *Thought and Change*, Chicago, University of Chicago Press.

GELLNER, E. (1983) *Nations and Nationalism*, Ithaca, Cornell University Press.

GLAZER, N. and MOYNIHAN, D. (eds.) (1975) *Ethnicity*, Cambridge, Harvard University Press.

GREEN, L. (1982) 'Rational Nationalists', *Political Studies*, 30, 2, pp. 236–247.

HANBY, V. (1976) 'The Renaissance of the S.N.P.: From Eccentric to Campaigning Crusader', in L. MAISEL (ed.) (1976) *Changing Campaign Techniques: Elections and Values in Contemporary Democracies*, Beverly Hills, Sage, pp. 217–241.

HANHAM, H. J. (1969) *Scottish Nationalism*, London, Faber and Faber.

HARGREAVE, P. (1969) *Scotland: The Third Choice*, London, Fabian Pamphet No. 392.

HARVIE, C. (1977) *Scotland and Nationalism: Scottish Society and Politics 1707–1977*, London, Allen and Unwin.

HECHTER, M. (1975) *Internal Colonialism: The Celtic Fringe in British National Development 1536–1966*, London, Routledge.

HECHTER, M. (1978) 'Group Formation and the Cultural Division of Labour', *American Journal of Sociology*, 84, 2, pp. 293–318.

HECHTER, M. and LEVI, M. (1979) 'The Comparative Analysis of Ethnoregional Movements', *Ethnic and Racial Studies*, 2, 3, 1979, pp. 260–274.

HERSHEY, M. J. (1974) *The Making of Campaign Strategy*, Massachusetts, Lexington.

HIBBS, D. A. (1977) 'Political Parties and Macroeconomic Policies', *American Political Science Review*' 71, 4, pp. 1467–87.

JACOBSEN, G. C. and KERNELL, S. (1981) *Strategy and Choice in Congressional Elections*, New Haven, Yale University Press.

JAENSCH, D. (1976) 'The Scottish Vote 1974: A realigning Party System?', *Political Studies*, 24, 3, pp. 306–319.

JUDGE, D. and FINDLAYSON, D. A. (1975) 'Scottish M.P.s: Problems of Devolution', *Parliamentary Affairs*, 28, 3, pp. 278–292.

KAVANAGH, D. A. (1970) *Constituency Electioneering in Britain*, London, Longmans.

KAUPPI, M. V. (1982) 'The Decline of the S.N.P.: Political and Organisational Factors', *Ethnic and Racial Studies*, 5, 3 pp. 326–48.

KEATING, M. J. and BLEIMAN, D. (1979) *Labour and Scottish Nationalism*, London, Macmillan.

KELLAS, J. G. (1976) 'Devolution in British Politics', paper delivered to the Political Studies Association, Nottingham.

KELLAS, J. G. (1980) *Modern Scotland*, London, Allen and Unwin.

KELLAS, J. G. (1989) *The Scottish Political System* (4th. Edn.), Cambridge, Cambridge University Press.

KENNEDY, G. (ed.) (1976) *The Radical Approach: Papers on an Independent Scotland*, Edinburgh, Palingenesis.

KESSEL, J. H. (1980) *Presidential Campaign Politics: Coalition Strategies and Citizens Response*, Homewood, Dorsey Press.

KOLINSKY, M. (ed.) (1979) *Divided Loyalties*, Manchester, Manchester University Press.

LATOUCHE, D. (1978) *Une Société de l'Ambiguité*, Montréal, Boréal Express.

LAVER, M. (1981) *The Politics of Private Desires*, Harmondsworth, Penguin.

LEE, G. (1976) 'North Sea Oil and Scottish Nationalism', *Political Quarterly*, 47, 3, pp. 307–317.

LEVY, R. (1982) 'The Non-Mobilisation of a Thesis: A Reply to Mughan and McAllister', *Ethnic and Racial Studies*, 5, 3, 1982, pp. 366–373.

LEVY, R. (1986) 'The Search for a Rational Strategy: The S.N.P. and Devolution 1974–79', *Political Studies*, 34, 3, pp. 236–248.

LEVY, R. (1988) 'Third Party Decline in the U.K.: The S.N.P. and the S.D.P. in Comparative Perspective', *West European Politics*, 11, 3, pp. 57–74.

LEVY, R. and GEEKIE, J. (1989) 'Devolution and the Tartanisation of the Labour Party', *Parliamentary Affairs*, 42, 3, pp. 399–411.

LUEBBERT, G. M. (1984) 'A Theory of Government Formation', *Comparative Political Studies*, 17, 2, pp. 229–264.

MCALLISTER, I. (1981) 'Party Organisation and Minority nationalism: A Comparative Study in the U.K.', *European Journal of Political Research*, 9, pp. 233–256.

MCCRONE, G. (1969) *Scotland's Future: The Economics of Nationalism*, Oxford, Blackwell.

MCKAY, D. (1980) *Scotland: Framework for Change*, Edinburgh, Paul Harris.

MACKINTOSH, J. P. (1967) 'Scottish Nationalism', *Political Quarterly*, 38, 4, pp. 389–402.

MACKINTOSH, J. P. (1968) *The Devolution of Power*, Harmondsworth, Penguin.

MCLAREN, A. A. (ed.) (1976) *Social Class in Scotland*, Edinburgh, John Donald.

MCLEAN, C. (ed.) (1979) *The Crown and the Thistle*, Edinburgh, Scottish Academic Press.

MCLEAN, I. (1970) 'The Rise and Fall of the S.N.P.', *Political Studies*, 18, 3, pp. 357–372.

MCLEAN, I. (1976) 'Devolution', *Political Quarterly*, 47, 2, pp. 221–227.

MCLEAN, I. (1977) 'The Politics of Nationalism and Devolution', *Political Studies* 25, 3.

MCLEAN, I. (1982) *Dealing in Votes: Interactions between Politicians and Voters in Britain and the USA*, Oxford, Martin Robertson.

MACRIDIS, R. (ed.) (1967) *Political Parties: Contemporary Trends and Ideas*, New York, Harper.

MAISEL, L. and COOPER, J. (eds.) (1978) *Political Parties, Development and Decay*, Beverly Hills, Sage.

MANSBACH, R. W. (1973) 'The S.N.P.: A Revised Political Profile', *Comparative Politics*, 5, 2, pp. 185–210.

MAUSER, G. (1983) *Political Marketing: An Approach to Campaign Strategy*, New York, Praeger.

MEADOWS, M. (1977) 'Constitutional Crisis in the UK: Scotland and the Devolution Controversey', *Review of Politics*, 39, 1, pp. 41–59.

MELSON, R. and WOLPE, H. (1970) 'Modernisation and the Politics of Communalism: A Theoretical Perspective', *American Political Science Review*, 64, p. 1112–1130.

MENY, Y. and WRIGHT, V. (eds.) (1985) *Centre-Periphery Relations in Western Europe*, London, Unwin.

MERCER, J. (1978) *Scotland: The Devolution of Power*, London, Calder.

MERKL, P. (1980) *Western European Party Systems: Trends and Perspectives*, New York, Free Press.

MILLER, K. (ed.) (1970) *Memoirs of a Modern Scotland*, London, Faber and Faber.

MILLER, W. (1977) *Electoral Dynamics in Britain since 1918*, London, Macmillan.

MILLER, W. (1979) *What Was the Profit in Following the Crowd? The Effectiveness of Party Strategy on Immigration and Devolution*, Glasgow, Centre for the Study of Public Policy.

MILLER, W., BRAND, J. and JORDAN, M. (1980) *Oil and the Scottish Voter 1974–79*, London, Social Science Research Council.

MILLER, W. (1981) *The End of British Politics: Scots and English Political Behaviour in the Seventies*, Oxford, Oxford University Press.

MISHLER, W. and MUGHAN, A. (1978) 'Representing the Celtic Fringe: Devolution and Legislative Behaviour in Scotland and Wales', *Legislative Studies Quarterly*, 3, 3, pp. 377–408.

MUGHAN, A. and MCALLISTER, I. (1981) 'The Mobilisation of the Ethnic Vote: A Thesis With Some Scottish and Welsh Evidence', *Ethnic and Racial Studies*, 4, 2, pp. 189–204.

MULLIN, W. A. R. (1979) 'The Scottish National Party', in H. M. DRUCKER (ed.) *Multi-Party Britain*, London, Macmillan.

NAIRN, T. (1981) *The Break-Up of Britain: Crisis and Neo-Nationalism*, London, New Left Books.

ORRIDGE, A. W. (1981) 'Uneven Development and Nationalism, pts. I and II', *Political Studies* 29, 1, pp. 1–15 and 29, 2, pp. 181–190.

O'SULLIVAN, C. (1986) *First World Nationalism: Class and Ethnic Politics in Northern Ireland and Quebec*, Chicago, University of Chicago Press.

PAGE, E. (1978) 'Michael Hechter's Internal Colonialism Thesis: Some Theoretical and Methodological Problems', *European Journal of Political Research*, 6, 3, pp. 295–317.

PARRY, R. (1988) *Scottish Political Facts*, Edinburgh, T. & T. Clark.

PARSLER, R. (ed.) (1980) *Capitalism, Class and Politics in Scotland*, Farnborough, Gower.

PERMAN, R. (1979) 'The Devolution Referendum Campaign of 1979', in H. and N. DRUCKER (eds.) *Scottish Government Yearbook 1980*, Edinburgh, Paul Harris.

PINARD, M. (1971) *The Rise of the Third Party: A Study in Crisis Politics*, Englewood Cliffs, Prentice Hall.

RABUSHKA, A. and SHEPSLE, K. A. (1972) *Politics in Plural Societies: A Theory of Democratic Instability*, Ohio, Merrill and Co.

RAGIN, C. C. (1977) 'Status and "Reactive Ethnic Cleavages" ', *American Sociological Review*, 42, pp. 438–450.

RAWKINS, P. (1978) 'Outsiders or Insiders: The Implications of Minority Nationalism in Scotland and Wales', *Comparative Politics*, 10, 4, pp. 519–534.

REID, G. (1976) *Devolution: A Guide*, Edinburgh, S.N.P. Publications.

RIKER, W. (1962) *A Theory of Political Coalitions*, New Haven, Yale University Press.

RIKER, W. and ORDESHOOK, P. (1973) *Positive Political Theory*, New Jersey, Prentice Hall.

RIKER, W. (1982) *Liberalism Against Populism: A Confrontation Between the Theory of Democracy and the Theory of Social Choice*, San Francisco, Freeman.

ROBERTSON, D. (1976) *A Theory of Party Competition*, New York, Wiley.

ROSE, R (1964), 'Parties, Factions and Tendencies in Britain', *Political Studies*, 12, 1, pp. 33–46.

ROSE, R. (1967) *Influencing Voters: A Study of Campaign Rationality*, London, Faber and Faber.

ROSE, R. (ed.) (1982) *Challenge to Governance*, London, Sage.

ROSE, R. (1984) *Do Parties Make a Difference?*, London, Macmillan.

ROSE, R. and MACKIE, T. (1984) *Do Parties Persist or Disappear? The Big Trade-Off Facing Organisations*, Glasgow, Centre for the Study of Public Policy, no. 134.

ROSE, R. and MCALLISTER, I. (1986) *Voters Begin to Choose*, London, Sage.

ROSENSTONE, S., BEHR, R. and LAZARUS, E. (1984) *Third Parties in America: Citizen Response to Major Party Failure*, New Jersey, Princeton University Press.

SARTORI, G. (1976) *Parties and Party Systems: A Framework for Analysis*, Cambridge, Cambridge University Press.

SCHATTSCHNEIDER, E. E. (1942) *Party Government*, New York, Holt, Reinhart.

SMELSER, N. (1963) *The Theory of Collective Behaviour*, Glencoe, Free Press.

SMITH, A. D. (1971) *Theories of Nationalism*, London, Duckworth.

SMITH, A. D. (1979) *Nationalism in the Twentieth Century*, New York, New York University Press.

SMITH, A. D. (1981) *The Ethnic Revival*, Cambridge, Cambridge University Press.

STUART, J. G. (1978) *The Mind Benders: Gradual Revolution and Scottish Independence*, Glasgow, McLellan.

STUDLAR, D. and McALLISTER, I. (1988) 'Nationalism in Scotland: A Post-Industrial Phenomenon?' *Ethnic and Racial Studies*, 11, 1, pp. 48–62.

THOMPSON, R. J. (1978) 'The S.N.P.: Its Bases of Support 1949–78', *Historicus*, 1, pp. 44–81.

TRUMAN, D. (1984) 'Party Reform, Party Atrophy and Constitutional Change', *Political Science Quarterly*, 99, 4, pp. 637–655.

URWIN, D. (1979) *Politics, Cultural Identity and Economic Expectations in Scotland*, Bergen, University of Bergen, Institute of Sociological and Political Studies.

VON BEYME, K. (1985) *Political Parties in Western Democracies*, Aldershot, Gower.

WALDMAN, S. R. (1972) *Foundations of Political Action: An Exchange Theory of Politics*, Boston, Little, Brown.

WEBB, K. (1978) *The Growth of Nationalism in Scotland*, Harmondsworth, Penguin.

WELLHOFER, E. S. (1972) 'Dimensions of Party Development: A Study in Organisational Dynamics', *Journal of Politics*, 34, 1, pp. 153–182.

WELLHOFER, E. S. (1979) 'Strategies for Party Organisation and Voter Mobilisation: Britain, Norway and Argentina', *Comparative Political Studies*, 12, 2, pp. 169–203.

WOLFE, J. N. (ed.) (1969) *Government and Nationalism in Scotland*, Edinburgh, Edinburgh University Press.

WOOD, J. R. (1981) 'Secession: A Comparative Analytical Framework', *Canadian Journal of Political Science*, 14, 1, pp. 107–134.

Index

152